THE LIVING THOUGHTS OF THE PROPHET MUHAMMAD

THE LIVING THOUGHTS
OF THE PROPHET
MUHAMMAD

Maulana Muḥammad 'Ali

THE LIVING THOUGHTS OF THE PROPHET MUHAMMAD

Maulana Muḥammad 'Ali

AUTHOR OF

an *English Translation of the Holy Qur'ān with Commentary* (with Arabic text), *The Religion of Islam, Muḥammad the Prophet, Early Caliphate, Living Thoughts of the Prophet Muḥammad, The Babi Movement, A Manual of Hadith* (English); *Bayan al-Qur'ān* - Urdu Translation and Commentary of the Qur'ān in three volumes, *Fadl al-Bari* Translation and Commentary of *al-Ṣaḥiḥ al-Buḵẖari* (Urdu), etc.

Published in U.S.A. by

Ahmadiyya Anjuman Ishaat Islam (Lahore) U.S.A.
P.O. Box 3370, Dublin, OH 43016-0176, U.S.A.

1992

First Published 1947

Copyright © 1992

Ahmadiyya Anjuman Ishaat Islam (Lahore) U.S.A.
P.O. Box 3370, Dublin, OH 43016-0176, U.S.A.

The Ahmadiyya Anjuman I<u>sh</u>ā'at Islām *(Ahmadiyya Society for the propagation of Islām)*, based in Lahore, Pakistan, is an international Muslim body devoted to the presentation of Islām through literary and missionary work. Since its inception in 1914, it has produced a range of highly acclaimed, standard books on all aspects of Islām, and has run Muslim missions in many parts of the world, establishing the first ever Islāmic centres in England (at Woking) and Germany (Berlin). The literature produced by the Anjuman, largely written by Maulana Muhammad Ali, is deep research work of the highest quality, based purely on the original sources of Islām. It has corrected many wrong notions about the religion of Islām, and has received world wide acclaim for its authenticity, scholarship and service of the faith.

Continuing the mission of Ḥaḍrat Mirza <u>Gh</u>ulām Aḥmad, the mujaddid of the 14th century Hijra and promised messiah, the Ahmadiyya Anjuman seeks to revive the original liberal, tolerant and rational spirit of Islām. It presents Islām as a great spiritual force for bringing about the moral reform of mankind, and shows that this religion has never advocated coercion, the use of physical force or the pursuit of political power in its support.

Information, books and free literature on Islām may be obtained by contacting *The Ahmadiyya Anjuman Ishā'at Islām Lahore* (or A.A.I.I.L.) at 1315 Kingsgate Road, Columbus, Ohio 43221 U.S.A.

Typsetting   Keywest Dataswitch Ltd.

Printers   Payette & Simms
            300 Arran Street
            St. Lambert, PQ
            Canada

Library of Congress card catalog number: 91-76110
                           ISBN: 0-913321-19-2

Contents

Transliteration v

Prefatory Note vi

A Brief Sketch of the Prophet's Life 1

Faith in God 42

The Oneness of Humanity 62

The Dignity of Manhood 69

Prayer to God 78

The Service of Humanity 88

Charity 93

Character Building 98

Wealth 112

Work and Labour 125

Home Life 131

The State 143

Transliteration

Below is explained the system of transliteration of proper names and Arabic words as adopted in this book. It follows the most recent rules recognized by European Orientalists with very slight variations.

’   stands for *hamza*, sounding like *h* in *hour*, a sort of catch in voice.

‘   stands for *'ain*, sounding like a strong guttural *hamza*.

a   sounds like *u* in *tub*.

ā   sounds like *a* in *father*

ai   sounds like *a* in *mat*; it represents a *fatha* before *yā*.

au   sounds between *au* in *auto* and *o* in *more*; it represents a *fatha* before *wāw*.

d   stands for *dāl*, being softer than *d*.

ḍ   stands for *ḍād*, sounding between *d* and *z*.

gh   stands for *ghain* (soft guttural *g*).

h   sounds like *h* in *how*.

ḥ   smooth guttural aspirate, sounds like *h* but is sharper.

i   sounds as *i* in *pin*

ī   sounds as *ee* in *deep*.

j   sounds as *g* in *gem*.

kh   stands for *khā*, sounds like *ch* in the Scotch word *loch*.

q   stands for *qaf*, strongly articulated guttural *k*.

ṣ   stands for *sad*, strongly articulated, like *s* in *hiss*.

sh   stands for *shīn*, sounding like *sh* in *she*.

t   sounds like Italian dental, softer than *t*.

ṭ   strongly articulated palatal *t*.

th   sounds between *th* in *thing* and *s*.

u   sounds like *u* in *pull*.

ū   sounds like *oo* in *moot*.

ẓ   strongly articulated palatal *z*.

Other letters sound as in English.

Prefatory Note

The following brief sketch of the life of the Prophet Muḥammad, the refomation he brought about and the great ideas which he gave to the world are based almost entirely on the Holy Quran. The Prophet's best-known name is Muḥammad, which means *the praised one*. Another name by which he was known is Aḥmad which means *the praising one*. The Quran, properly Qur'ān, is the name of the Scripture which the Prophet claimed to have been revealed to him by God. This too is a significant name, and means *what is* or *should be read* or *recited*. The name of the religion which the Prophet preached is Islām, which again is a significant name and means *entering into peace*; the follower of this religion is called a Muslim, which means *one who has found peace*. The terms Muhammadan and Muhammadanism have never been in vogue among the followers of this religion.

The Holy Quran was revealed to the Prophet piecemeal during a period of twenty-three years, from the fortieth year of his life to his death. It is divided into 114 chapters, each chapter being called a *sūra*. The larger chapters are sub-divided into sections, each section being called a *ruk'u*. Each chapter consists of a number of verses. The chapters are of unequal length, the longest chapter containing about one-twelfth of the entire book while the smallest contains only three verses. Some of the chapters were revealed entire, but the revelation of the majority of the larger chapters extended over years, and some of the smaller ones were also revealed in pieces. When a chapter was revealed in parts, the Prophet specified the place of the verse or verses revealed. Thus the arrangement of the verses in each chapter was entirely his own. The arrangement of the chapters was also the Prophet's own work. Every part revealed was both written down and committed to memory, as soon as it was revealed, by the Prophet's companions. The whole of the Quran according to the Prophet's arrangement was safe in the memories of men in the Prophet's life-time, while the written manuscripts were gathered together immediately after his death, by the orders of Abū Bakr, his first successor. Therefore, all Muslims wherever they may be living have the same Quran.

About two-thirds of the Holy Quran was revealed at Mecca where the Prophet passed thirteen years of his life after the Call, and about one-third at Medina where he passed the last ten years of his life. In arrangement the chapters revealed at Mecca are intermixed with those revealed at Medina. The following table will give the reader an approximate idea of the historical order of revelation of the chapters as they stand in the present arrangement:

Early Mecca period	60 chapters: 1, 17-21, 50-56, 67-109, 111-114.
Middle Mecca period	17 chapters: 29-32, 34-39, 40-46.
Last Mecca period	15 chapters: 6, 7, 10-16, 22, 23, 25-28.
Early Medina period	6 chapters: 2, 8, 47, 61, 62, 64.
Middle Medina period	12 chapters: 3-5, 24, 33, 48, 57-60, 63, 65.
Last Medina period	4 chapters: 9, 49, 66, 110.

The Holy Quran is the chief, and admittedly the most reliable, source of the Prophet's teachings, the principles being all laid down in it. Sunna (lit., a *way* or *rule* or *manner of acting*), which means the Prophet's practice, is a secondary source of what the Prophet taught. Ḥadīth literally means *a saying*, but in its technical sense it is the narration or record of Sunna. In effect Sunna and Ḥadīth cover the same ground and are applicable to the Prophet's actions, practices and sayings, but Ḥadīth is a wider term as it contains, in addition to the record of the Prophet's practices, prophetical and historical elements. Sunna or Ḥadīth was recognized from the very beginning as affording guidance in religious matters, and its need, its force as law and its preservation are all traceable to the life-time of the Prophet, though undoubtedly Ḥadīth collections in book form came later.

The collection of Ḥadīth passed through five stages before it assumed the form of *Musnad* and *Jami'*. The latter brings the knowledge of Ḥadīth to perfection, and it not only arranges reports according to their subject matter, which is not the case with Musnad, but is also of a more critical tone. Six collections of Ḥadīth are recognized in this class by the Ahl Sunna as reliable, commonly known as Bukhārī, Muslim, Abū Dāwūd, Tirmidhī, Ibn Māja and Nasā'ī. Of these Bukhārī which is the first in point of time is the most critical also, and undoubtedly occupies the first place in reliability. In this treatise Bukhārī has been referred to more frequently than any other collection. Occasionally the Mishkāt, which is a collection of Ḥadīth taken from the above six books and some other collections, such as Baihaqī, Dar Qutnī, etc., and has been translated into English, has also been referred to.

All references given in this treatise without an indication of the name are to the Holy Quran, the first figure representing the number of the chapter and the second figure the number of the verse. All other references are indicated by name. In the reference to Ḥadīth collections, the first figure represents the number of the book and the second the number of the chapter.

MUHAMMAD ALI

MUSLIM TOWN,
LAHORE, INDIA.
3.12.46.

Chapter 1
A Brief Sketch of the Prophet's Life

It was in the year 571 of the Christian Era that the Prophet Muḥammad was born, on the 12th of the lunar month Rabīʻl. He came of the noblest family of Arabia, the Quraish, who were held in the highest esteem, being guardians of the Sacred House at Mecca, the Kaʻba, the spiritual centre of the whole of Arabia. At the time of his birth Arabia was steeped deep in the worst form of idolatry that has ever prevailed in any country. The Kaʻba itself was full of idols, and every household had, in addition, its own idols. Unhewn stones, trees and heaps of sand were also worshipped. In spite of this vast and deep-rooted idolatry, the Arabs were, as Bosworth Smith remarks, materialistic. "Eat and drink is," as he says, "the epicurean tone of the majority of the poems that have come down to us." There was practically no faith in the life after death, no feeling of responsibility for one's actions. The Arabs, however, believed in demons, and diseases were attributed to the influence of evil spirits. Ignorance prevailed among the high as well as the low, so much so that the noblest of men could boast of his ignorance. There was no moral code, and vice was rampant. The sexual relations were loose. Obscene poems and songs were recited in public assemblies. There was no punishment for adultery, nor any moral sanction against it. Prostitution had nothing dishonourable about it, so that leading men could keep brothels. Women were "in the most degraded position, worse even than that in which they were under the laws of Manu in Hindustan."[1] Woman was looked on as a mere chattel. Instead of having any right to inheritance of property, her own person formed

---

1. Bosworth Smith

1

part of the inheritance, and the heir could dispose of her as he liked, even if he did not care to take her as a wife. There was no settled government, no law in the land, and might was practically right. The Arabs belonged to one race and spoke one language, yet they were the most disunited people. Tribe made war on tribe, and family on family, on the most trivial excuse. The strong among them trampled upon the rights of the weak, and the weak could not get their wrongs redressed. The widow and the orphan were quite helpless and slaves were treated most cruelly.

Amongst this people was born Muḥammad, an orphan from his birth, who lost even his mother when six years old. He came of the noblest family of the Quraish, yet, like the rest of his countrymen, he was not taught reading and writing. He tended sheep for some time, and the noblest of the Arabs had no contempt for that occupation, but in his youth he was chiefly occupied in trade. It was, however, his high morals that distinguished him from the first from all his compatriots. The Holy Quran, which contains the most trustworthy account of the Prophet's life, says that he was the "possessor of sublime morals."[2] Leading generally a reserved life, he had for friends only those men whose moral greatness was admitted by all. His truthfulness is testified in the clearest words.[3] His bitterest opponents were challenged to point out a single black spot on his character during the forty years that he had passed among them before he received the Divine call.[4] It was in his youth that, on account of his pure and unsoiled character and his love for truth and honesty, he won from his compatriots the title of al-Amīn, or the Faithful. Living in a country in which idol-worship was the basis of the everyday life of the community, Muḥammad hated idolatry from his childhood, and the Holy Quran is again our authority for the statement that he never bent his forehead before an idol.[5] Even Sir William Muir bears testimony to the purity of his character in his youth: "Our authorities all agree in ascribing to the youth of Muḥammad a modesty of deportment and purity of manners rare among the Meccans." And again: "Endowed with a refined mind and

---

2.   68:4   3.   6:33   4.   10:16   5.   109:4

delicate taste, reserved and meditative, he lived much within himself, and the pondering of his heart no doubt supplied occupation for leisure hours spent by others of a low stamp in rude sports and profligacy. The fair character and honourable bearings of the unobtrusive youth won the approbation of his fellow-citizens: and by common consent he received the title of *al-Amīn* the Faithful."

Though he lived in a city in which drinking orgies were only too common, never did a drop of wine touch his lips. Even Abū Bakr, the most intimate friend of Muḥammad's youth, never tasted wine. The society at Mecca found pleasure in gambling, yet never did Muḥammad take part in any such pastime. He lived among a people who were addicted to war as they were addicted to wine, yet he had no liking for either.

To quote Muir again, "though now nearly twenty years of age he had not acquired the love of arms." Perforce, he had to take part on one occasion in the famous sacrilegious war that continued for four years between the Quraish and the Hawāzin, yet he did no more than gather up arrows that came from the enemy and hand them over to his uncles. He did not even take to trading for love of wealth but simply out of regard for his uncle Abū Ṭālib, whom he loved to help. Thus says Muir: "Muḥammad was never covetous of wealth, or at any period of his career energetic in the pursuit of riches for their own sake. If left to himself, he would probably have preferred the quiet and repose of his present life to the bustle and cares of a mercantile journey. He would not spontaneously have contemplated such an expedition. But when the proposal was made, his generous soul at once felt the necessity of doing all that was possible to relieve his uncle and he cheerfully responded to the call."

Above all, his earlier life was marked by that rare characteristic, rarest of all in Arabia at the time, love of the poor, the orphan, the widow, the weak, the helpless and the slave. Before he had affluence of means, he was one of the members who took an oath to stand by the oppressed and formed themselves into a league as champions of the injured. When at twenty-five he married a wealthy widow, Khadīja, he spent freely for the help of the poor. No slave came into the household but was set free by him. He had acquired such a fame for helping the poor that when, after the Call, the Quraish demanded him of Abū Ṭālib to put him to death, the old chief refused and praised him in a poem as the "Protector of the orphans and the widows." Earlier than this when Muḥammad received the Call, and was diffident whether he would be able to achieve the grand object of reforming his countrymen, his wife, Khadīja, comforted him, saying that "God would not disgrace him because he bore the burden of those who were weary and helped the poor and gave relief to those who were in distress and honoured the guest and loved his kinsmen."[6]

To these great qualities was added his anxiety for a fallen humanity. The Quran refers to it repeatedly.[7] As years went on, the gross idolatry of the Arabs and their evil ways pressed the more heavily on his heart, and he spent hours in solitude in the neighbouring mountains. Still later, he repaired for days to a cave at the foot of Mount Ḥirā, and it was here that the Divine light shone on him in its full resplendence. At first, he was in doubt whether he would be able to perform the great task, but his anxiety soon gave place to absolute faith that truth would ultimately triumph, and he set to work with a strength of will and an inflexibility of purpose which could not be shaken by the severest opposition of the whole of Arabia. From the very first his message was for all, for the Arab as well as the non-Arab, for the idolaters as well as the Jews, the Christians and the Magi. Nor was it limited to the town of Mecca, for Mecca was the centre to which men and women flocked in thousands every year from all parts of Arabia, and through this assemblage the Prophet's message reached the most distant corners of Arabia. His wife, Khadīja, was the first to believe in him, and she was followed by others who were either his most intimate friends or closely related to him. As Muir remarks: "It is strongly corroborative of Muḥammad's sincerity that the earliest converts to Islām were not only of upright character, but his own bosom friends and people of his household, who, intimately acquainted with his private life, could not fail otherwise to have detected those discrepancies which ever

---

6.   Bukhārī, I:I   7.   9:128; 18:6; 26:3; 35:8

more or less exist between the professions of the hypocritical deceiver abroad and his actions at home."

His first revelations laid stress on the great power and majesty of the Divine Being and on the inevitability of the judgment. The Quraish mocked at first, treated him contemptuously and called him a madman. In spite of this he went on gaining adherents by twos and threes, until within four years the number reached forty and persecution grew bitter. At first the slaves were tortured, Bilāl, a Negro by birth, when made to lie on the burning sands under the Arabian midday sun continued to cry, "One, One," to the bewilderment of his persecutors. But the fire of persecution once kindled could not be confined. Converts of high birth were made to suffer along with the poorer followers. The Prophet himself did not escape the cruelties of the persecutors. The Muslims could not gather together or say their prayers in a public place. Still Muḥammad went on gaining new adherents, and his opponents became severer in their persecution, so much so that some of the humbler converts were put to death in a most brutal manner. The Prophet's tender heart melted at the sight of this brutal treatment of innocent men and women, and in spite of the fact that he would be left alone amongst exasperated opponents, he advised the small band of his followers to betake themselves to a place of safety. Eleven men and women left Mecca in the fifth year of the Hijra, and migrated to Abyssinia. Thither they were followed by a deputation of their opponents that petitioned the ruler of Abyssinia for their extradition. The Muslim case was put by their leader before the king as follows:

> O King! We were an ignorant people, given to idolatry. We used to eat corpses even of animals that died a natural death, and to do all sorts of disgraceful things. We did not make good our obligations to our relations, and we ill-treated our neighbours. The strong among us would thrive at the expense of the weak, till at last Allāh raised a Prophet for our reformation. His descent, his righteousness, his integrity and his virtue are well known to us. He called us to the worship of Allāh, and bade us give up idolatry and stone-worship. He enjoined on us to tell the truth, to make good

our trust, to have regard for our kith and kin, and to do good to our neighbours. He taught us to shun everything foul and to avoid bloodshed. He forbade all sorts of indecent things, telling lies and misappropriating orphans' belongings. So we believed in him, followed him and acted up to his teachings. Thereupon our people began to do us wrong, to subject us to tortures, thinking that we might abjure our faith and revert to idolatry. When, however, their cruelties exceeded all bounds, we came to seek an asylum in your country.

The Negus was deeply touched by this statement and by a recitation from the Holy Quran, and refused to deliver the Muslims to their enemies. More Muslims went to Abyssinia next year, until the total reached 101, excluding children. The Quraish tried their utmost to check this tide of emigration, but in vain. Soon they became exasperated beyond all measure at the Prophet and the little band of Muslims that remained with him at Mecca. Not being able to prevail upon Abū Ṭālib, the head of the Hashimites (the Prophet's family), to hand the Prophet over to them to end his life, and failing to tempt the Prophet by offering him kingship, wealth and beauty, they at last entered into a league and shut up the Hashimites and the Muslims in a small quarter, where they suffered the utmost privations for three long years, being allowed liberty of action only during the time of pilgrimage. These three years were the years of the hardest suffering for the Muslims, and Islām itself made little progress during this time.

Released at last from this imprisonment, the Prophet, though facing disappointment on all sides, had still as much faith in the triumph of the truth as ever. If Mecca was now quite deaf to his preaching, he would turn elsewhere. He went to Ṭā'if, another great city of Arabia. Here, however, he found the ground even harder than at Mecca. He was not allowed to stay in Ṭā'if after ten days, and as he walked back he was pelted with stones. Dripping with blood and not even allowed by his persecutors to take rest he at last returned to Mecca, a sadder man than when he had left it. But if men did not listen to him, yet would he open his heart to God who was always

ready to listen, and he prayed to Him thus when coming back from
Ṭā'if:

> O my God! To Thee I complain of the feebleness of my
> strength and of my lack of resourcefulness and of my
> insignificance in the eyes of people. Thou art the most
> Merciful of the merciful, Thou art the Lord of the weak. To
> whom wilt Thou entrust me, to an unsympathetic foe who
> would sullenly frown at me, or to a close friend to whom
> Thou has given control over my affair? Not in the least do I
> care for anything except that I may have Thy protection. In
> the light of Thy face do I seek shelter, in the light which
> illumines the heaven and dispels all sorts of darkness, and
> which controls all affairs in this world as well as in the
> Hereafter. May it never be that I should incur Thy wrath or
> that Thou shouldst be displeased with me. There is no
> strength, nor power, but in Thee.

He feels that no man lends his ear to his message, yet his faith in
the goodness of God and in the ultimate triumph of his cause is as
unshaken as ever. To him God is all in all and the opposition of the
whole world is as nothing. With marvellous calmness he undergoes
the severest hardships which he has to suffer for working for the
good of the very people who take pleasure in inflicting on him the
cruellest tortures. All these, he says, are insignificant so long as he
enjoys the pleasure of God. What a firm faith in God, what a cheerful
resignation to His supreme will, what an unalloyed spiritual
happiness!

Three years more passed away at Mecca amidst the most trying
circumstances. In the meanwhile Islām took root in Medina and
spread fast. As the thirteenth year of the Call drew to a close,
seventy-five Muslims (including two women) from Medina came to
perform a pilgrimage and swore allegiance to the Prophet, affirming
that if he chose to go to Medina, they would defend him against his
enemies just as they defended their own children and wives. Then it
was that the Muslim exodus to Medina commenced. The Prophet
chose to remain alone amidst an enemy that was growing more and
more exasperated, and to see his followers safe at the new centre.

This shows the depth of his love and concern for his followers. He was anxious more for their safety than for his own. Within two months, about 150 Muslims left Mecca and there remained only the Prophet with two of his closest friends. The psychological moment had now arrived for his enemies to deal the final blow. Individual efforts had hitherto been made to do away with the Prophet, but they had failed. If the final blow was not struck immediately, the Prophet might escape to Medina and get beyond their reach. A big conference of all the tribes was held and a final decision taken. A youth from each clan was to be selected, and all these were to fall upon the Prophet at one and the same time, so that no particular clan should be held accountable for the murder. The Prophet's house was besieged by these bloodthirsty youths as soon as it was dark, but, undaunted and having his faith in Divine protection, the Prophet passed through them unnoticed. In the dark of the night, with only one companion, he made his way through the streets of Mecca to the bare and rugged hills outside, and a hiding-place was ultimately found in a cave known as Thaur. When morning appeared, the enemy saw the failure of their plan and the whole countryside was scoured. One party reached the very mouth of the cave. Through a crevice, Abū Bakr saw the enemy at the mouth and grieved. "Do not grieve, for Allāh is with us," said the Prophet. The more helpless he became, the stronger grew his faith in God. And surely some invisible power saved him throughout his life every time that the enemy's hand was on him. After three days the Prophet and his companion started for Medina.

It was not the Prophet alone who bore all the hard trials so willingly at Mecca for thirteen years; those who accepted him bore persecutions with the same willing heart. The new life to which the Prophet had awakened them has drawn words of praise from Sir William Muir:

> The believers bore persecutions with a patient and tolerant spirit. ... One hundred men and women, rather than abjure their precious faith, had abandoned home and sought refuge, till the storm should be overpast, in Abyssinian exile. And now again a still larger number, with the Prophet himself,

were emigrating from their fondly loved city with its Sacred Temple, to them the holiest spot on earth, and fleeing to Medina. There, the same marvellous charm had within two or three years been preparing for them a brotherhood ready to defend the Prophet and his followers with their blood. Jewish truth had long sounded in the ears of the men of Medina; but it was not until they heard the spirit-stirring strains of the Arabian Prophet that they too awoke from their slumber and sprang suddenly into a new and earnest life.

The Prophet reached Medina on the 12th of Rabī'I, corresponding to June 28, 622 of the Christian Era. The first thing that he did on reaching Medina was to construct a mosque, now famous as the Prophet's Mosque. Here prayers to God were offered five times daily in a free atmosphere for the first time in the history of Islām. He next turned to establishing a brotherhood of the Muslims. Those who had fled from Mecca, called Muhājirs (Refugees), had left all their property behind. So, to provide shelter for them, every refugee was bound in a bond of brotherhood with one of the residents of Medina, called Anṣār (Helpers).

The third important matter to which the Prophet turned his attention was to establish friendly relations between the various tribes living in Medina. Among these were three Jewish clans, and a pact was concluded with them as well. The main terms of this pact were as follows: 1. The Muslims and the Jews shall live as one people. 2. Each one of the parties shall keep to its own faith. 3. In the event of a war with a third party, each shall be bound to come to the assistance of the other, provided the party at war were not the aggressors. 4. In the event of an attack on Medina, both shall join hands to defend it. 5. Peace shall be made after consultation with each other. 6. Medina shall be regarded as sacred by both, all bloodshed being forbidden therein. 7. The Prophet shall be the final court of appeal in cases of dispute. This agreement with the Jews shows that the Prophet had an apprehension that the exasperated Quraish who were foiled in their attempt to put an end to his life at Mecca would now attack Medina.

We have seen that when the Muslims fled to Abyssinia, the Quraish tried all the means in their power to have them expelled from there. How could they see Islām prosper so near home at Medina, an important city only 270 miles distant and on the trade route to Syria. Muḥammad had already received an intimation from on High that he would have to carry on a war to save Islām from utter annihilation. The sword, he was told, would be taken up against him and he would have to fight to save the small community of Islām from destruction at the hands of a powerful enemy who was determined to uproot Islām from the soil of Arabia. Temperamentally Muḥammad was not inclined to war; he had not once handled the sword in actual fighting up to the fifty-fifth year of his age, and this in a country where, owing to constant internecine warfare, fighting had become a vocation of the people. The religion which he preached, Islām, (lit. peace or submission), was a religion of peace, laying stress on prayer to God and the service of humanity, and he was required to preach this religion; to deliver the message, not to enforce it on others:

> The truth is from your Lord, so, whoever will, let him believe, and whoever will, let him disbelieve.[8]

> We have shown man the way, he may be thankful or he may be unthankful.[9]

And in still plainer words, it was laid down:

> There is no compulsion in religion.[10]

But war was being forced on him and it was his duty, he was told, to defend his oppressed community who had twice fled their homes from the persecutions of a cruel enemy to a distant place:

> Permission to fight is given to those upon whom war is made because they are oppressed, and Allāh is well able to help them.[11]

Why were they expelled from their homes? Why was war made on them? What was their offence?

---

8.   18:29   9.   76:3   10.   2:256   11.   22:39

Those who have been expelled from their homes without a just cause, except that they say, Our Lord is Allāh.[12]

To worship Allāh, to say that Allāh is our Lord, to bow before Him, was an offence in this land, the punishment for which was that the men who worshipped God, and the places where He was worshipped, should be destroyed. So the Muslims were required to defend all houses of worship, whether they belonged to the Jews or the Christians or their own community:

> And had there not been Allāh's repelling some people by means of others, cloisters and churches and synagogues and mosques in which Allāh's name is remembered most, would certainly have been pulled down.[13]

These three statements follow one another in the Divine revelation to the Prophet. In a later revelation he was further told that he should by no means resort to an aggressive war. It was in defence only that he was allowed to take up the sword:

> And fight in the way of Allāh with those who fight with you, and do not exceed this limit, for Allāh does not love those who exceed the limits.[14]

There was no question of converting anyone to Islām by force; it was the enemy that wanted to turn back the Muslims by force from Islām:

> And they will not cease fighting with you until they turn you back from your religion if they can.[15]

Religion was a matter between God and His servants and no one had a right to compel anyone to adopt a particular religion, and the Prophet had thus to fight for the noble cause of the liberty of man:

> And fight with them until there is no persecution and religion is held for Allāh. But if they give up persecution, then there should be no hostility except against the oppressors.[16]

---

12. 22:40   13. 22:40   14. 2:190   15. 2:217
16. 2:193

If the Prophet was required to cease fighting when the enemy ceased to persecute on account of religion, he was also required to cease fighting if the enemy offered peace, even though he might be gaining time only to renew his attack:

> And if they incline to peace, do thou also incline to it and trust in Allāh; He is the Hearing, the Knowing. And if they intend to deceive thee, then surely Allāh is sufficient for thee.[17]

It was in these circumstances and on these conditions that the Prophet was allowed to fight. He had not up to this time trained a single man for fighting; he had no army at all. He had a small community of followers trained only in praying to God, and even they could not be forced to fight. To carry on the war, even though single-handed, was his duty:

> Fight then in Allāh's way; this is not imposed on thee except in relation to thyself, and rouse the believers to ardour; maybe Allāh will restrain the fighting of those who disbelieve, and Allāh is strongest in prowess and strongest to punish (offenders).[18]

Small detachments of the Quraish used to go out on marauding expeditions and scour the country right up to the outskirts of Medina. The situation called for vigilance on the part of the Prophet. Reconnaissance parties were sent out by him to keep an eye on enemy movements and to approach certain tribes to secure their alliance or neutrality. One such party sent out with express orders to gather information about the Quraish movements accidentally killed a member of the Quraish, Ibn Hadzramī by name. The usual practice in Arabia in such cases was to demand blood-money. But the Quraish wanted a pretext to rouse the populace against the Muslims, and Ibn Hadzramī's murder furnished it. Another pretext was furnished by a Quraish caravan coming from Syria just at this time. Knowing that the Muslims were still very weak, the Quraish thought that 1000 men would be sufficient to annihilate them, and with this

---

17. 8:61, 62   18. 4:84

army they marched on Medina in the month of Ramadzān, the Muslim month of fasting, in the second year of the Prophet's Flight. When news of this reached Medina, the Prophet made hurried preparations to meet them, but could gather only a force of 313 Muslims. The two forces met at Badr, a distance of three days' journey from Medina and ten days' from Mecca; on the one side being 1000 veteran warriors with whom fighting had been a life-long profession, armed with every weapon of warfare of the time, and on the other only 313 ill-equipped men, including raw youths and men advanced in age. The Prophet saw this and in deep anxiety passed the night praying to God in a small hut: "O Allāh! Shouldst Thou suffer this small band of believers to perish this day, no one will be left on earth to worship Thee and carry Thy message to the world. O Living One! O Subsisting One by whom all subsist! I cry to Thee for Thy mercy."

The unexpected happened. Almost all the Quraish chiefs, the ringleaders of the campaign against Islām, were slain in action. Seeing their chiefs fall, the rank and file were seized with confusion and took to flight. Seventy fell and an equal number were taken prisoners. There were fourteen casualties on the Muslim side.

The Quraish defeat at Badr was an ignominy which they could not leave unavenged. An army of 3000 strong, with warriors like Khālid among them, marched on Medina next year, Shawwāl A.H. The Muslims could muster no more than 700 men, and marched out of Medina to meet the enemy at the foot of Uḥud, only three miles from the city. The Muslims fought desperately and seven of the enemy's flagbearers fell one after another. Utter confusion seized the Quraish. They took to flight and the Muslims pursued them, but just at this time Khālid saw that the Muslim archers had left their rear undefended by vacating a certain position to join in the pursuit, and wheeling round at the head of his 200 cavalry attacked the Muslims from behind. Seeing this, the fleeing Quraish army also turned back, and the handful of Muslims, in disorder on account of the pursuit, were thus pressed on both sides. The position was so precarious that the whole Muslim army was now in danger of being annihilated. The Prophet, braving the danger of himself becoming the target of the enemy's attack, called out aloud to his men to rally round him: "To me, O servants of Allāh! I am the Messenger of Allāh." This was a signal to the enemy to direct their attack to this particular point. The Muslims saw this and, cutting their way through the enemy ranks, mustered strongly round the Prophet. But in this attempt they sustained serious losses, and Muṣ'ab ibn 'Umair, who resembled the Prophet, being killed, the news spread like wildfire that the Prophet had been killed. Still the Muslims did not lose heart. "Let us fight on for the cause for which the Prophet fought," said one of them. By this time, the Prophet had sustained serious wounds and had fallen down, but the position had become secure both for the army and for the Prophet himself who was surrounded on all sides by devoted friends." Here closing their ranks on elevated ground with the mountain protecting their rear, they again made the enemy feel their strength. The Quraish retired from the field and took their way back to Mecca. When some one entreated the Prophet to pray for the destruction of his enemies he raised his hands, saying: "O Allāh! Forgive my people for they do not know."

Though they had this time inflicted severe losses on the Muslims, the Quraish knew that even this attack on Medina had proved abortive. Therefore, after returning from Uḥud, they tried to raise the Jews and the Bedouin tribes against the Muslims, and in this they were successful. The Jews, the Bedouins and the Quraish all combined to deal a crushing blow to Islām, A large army of 10,000 was gathered together in the fifth year of the Flight. The Muslims, unable to meet these hosts in the open field, fortified themselves in Medina by digging a ditch on the side which was unprotected. The Prophet himself participated in digging the ditch like an ordinary labourer. Covered with dust and with the fear of annihilation lurking in their minds, they yet sang in happy chorus:

> O Allāh! Had it not been for Thy mercy, we would not have been guided aright,
> Nor would we have given alms, nor would we have prayed to Thee.
> Send down tranquillity upon us and establish our steps in battle,

> For they are risen against us and they wish to pervert us by
> force — But we refuse, but we refuse.

The huge force at last reached Medina. It was an hour of
consternation for the Muslims. The Holy Quran thus depicts the
anguish and perplexity of the moment:

> When they came upon you from above you and from below
> you, and when the eyes turned dull and the hearts rose up to
> the throats, and some of you began to entertain diverse
> thoughts about Allāh. There the believers were sorely tried
> and shaken with a severe shaking.[19]

Amid this seeming scene of dread and terror, the hearts of the
Muslims were full of faith:

> And when the believers saw the Allies, they said: This is
> what Allāh and His Messenger promised us, and Allāh and
> His Messenger spoke the truth: and it only increased them in
> faith and submission.[20]

During a full month of siege the Muslims stood firm. Arrows and
stones came in terrible showers but they could not break through the
defence. Attacks were made and repulsed in quick succession. The
siege became wearisome to the besieging army, which also began to
run short of provisions. The elements of nature ultimately came to
the help of the brave Muslim defence. A storm raged one night which
blew down the tents of the besiegers. There was confusion among the
Allies and they took to flight during the night, to the great joy and
thanksgiving of the Muslims.

The Quraish now lost all hope of being able to crush the
Muslims. About a year after this, the Prophet with about 1400
companions (Islām was gaining ground in spite of the wars)
undertook a journey to Mecca to perform the lesser pilgrimage, but
finding that the Quraish were prepared to offer armed resistance to
his entry into Mecca, even though it was simply with the object of
performing a religious obligation, he had to stop at about nine miles

---

19. 33:10, 11   20. 33:22

from the sacred city, at a place called Ḥudaibiya. Emissaries were sent to find a peaceful solution, but they were maltreated, and at last a man of the high position of 'Uthman, deputed to negotiate, was arrested by the Quraish. The situation was critical; the Muslim envoy had been taken into custody and there was a rumour that he had been murdered. The Muslims were unarmed except for sheathed swords, which they carried as a necessity when journeying in a country like Arabia, but they were determined not to turn their backs. The Prophet took a pledge from them, and they pledged afresh one and all, that they would fight to the last man in defence of the Prophet, whom the enemy wanted to put to death. This pledge is known as *Bai'ak al-Ridzwān* (Pledge of Divine Pleasure) in the history of Islām.

This resolve on the part of the Muslims brought the Quraish to their senses and a truce was at last drawn up to last for a period of ten years, with the following conditions among others:

1.   The Muslims shall return without performing a pilgrimage, for which they may come back the following year.

2.   Should any of the Meccans go over to Medina, the Muslims shall hand him over to the Meccans, but if any of the Muslims go over to Mecca, the Quraish are under no obligation to return him to the Muslims.

3.   The Arab tribes are at liberty to enter into alliance with whichever party they choose.

It can easily be seen what a heavy price the Prophet was willing to pay for the sake of peace; he had agreed not to give shelter to those who were persecuted for accepting Islām, while his own men were free to join the unbelievers and find shelter in Mecca. The moral force drawing the people to Islām was so great that while not a single Muslim went back to Mecca where he could find a sure shelter, scores of Meccans embraced Islām, and finding the doors of Medina closed to them, settled themselves at 'Īs, a place subject neither to the authority of the Prophet, nor to that of the Quraish. Islām was spreading in spite of the sword.

After returning from Ḥudaibiya, the Prophet made arrangements to send the message of Islām to all people, Christians as well as Magians, living on the borders of Arabia. He wrote letters to the sovereigns of the neighbouring kingdoms, the Emperor of Rome, Chosreos II of Persia, the king of Egypt, the Negus of Abyssinia, and certain Arab chiefs, inviting them to Islām. The letter to the Roman Emperor was worded as follows:

> In the name of Allāh, the Beneficent, the Merciful. From Muḥammad, the servant of Allāh and His Messenger, to Heraclius, the chief of the Romans. Peace be with him who follows the guidance. After this, I invite thee with invitation to Islām. Become a Muslim and thou wilt be in peace - Allāh will give thee a double reward; but if thou turnest away, on thee will be the sin of thy subjects. And, O followers of the Book! Come to an equitable proposition between us and you that we shall not serve any but Allāh, and that we shall not associate aught with Him and that some of us shall not take others for lords besides Allāh; but if they turn back, then say: Bear witness that we are Muslims.[21]

Of the rulers addressed the Negus accepted Islām; the king of Egypt sent some presents in reply; the Roman Emperor was impressed but his generals were averse; while Chosroes tore up the letter and sent orders to the governor of Yemen to arrest the Prophet. When the governor's soldiers reached Medina for the execution of the orders, the Prophet told them that Chosroes was himself dead and no more the king of Persia. They went back with this report to the governor of Yemen and it was found that Chosroes II had actually been murdered by his own son on the very night indicated by the Prophet. This event led to the governor's conversion to Islām, and ultimately to Yemen's throwing off the yoke of Persia.

The truce of Ḥudaibiya had hardly been in force for two years when the Banū Bakr, an ally of the Quraish, attacked the Khuzā'a an ally of the Muslims, with the help of the Quraish. The Prophet

---

21. Bukhārī, I:I

thereupon sent word to the Quraish that they should either pay blood-money for those slain from among the Khuzā'a or dissociate themselves from the Banū Bakr, or, in the last resort, declare the truce of Hudaibiya to be null and void. The Quraish did not agree to either of the first two proposals, and the result was the annulment of the truce. The Prophet thereupon ordered an attack on Mecca in the closing months of the eighth year of the Flight. The two years during which the truce remained in force had brought such large numbers over to Islām that the Prophet now marched on Mecca with 10,000 men under his flag. The Meccans were unable to make any preparations to meet the attack. At Marr al-Zahrān, a day's journey from Mecca, the Quraish leader, Abū Sufyān, sued for pardon, and though he was the arch-offender who had left no stone unturned to annihilate Islām, free pardon was granted to him by the Prophet.

The conquest of Mecca was practically bloodless. The Quraish were unable to meet this force and the Prophet declared a general amnesty, guaranteeing safety to all those who entered Abū Sufyān's house, or closed the doors of their own houses or entered the sacred precincts of the Ka'ba. Conversion to Islām formed no part of the conditions which guaranteed security of life and property. There were strict orders to the advancing army that there should be no bloodshed. There were only about a score of casualties due to 'Ikrima, son of Abū Jahl, attacking a part of the Muslim forces under Khālid, who was now a Muslim.

Mecca having thus been entered, the first thing that the Prophet did was to clear the Ka'ba of the idols. He then addressed the assembled Quraish who had been guilty of the most heinous offences against the Muslims. They were standing before him now as culprits who had persecuted Muslims, inflicted on them the severest tortures, put many of them to death and ultimately expelled them from Mecca. They had not even allowed the Muslims to live a peaceful life at their new home in Medina, but had attacked that city thrice with large forces which they knew the Muslims had no means to meet. It was these men who were now at the Prophet's mercy, and addressing them, he put to them the question: "What treatment do you expect from me?"

They knew *al-Amīn* of old; they knew Muḥammad had a generous heart within his breast. "Thou art a noble brother, the son of a noble brother," was their unhesitating reply. But the treatment Muḥammad accorded them exceeded even their own expectations. "This day," he said in the words of Joseph to his brothers, "there is no reproof against you."[22] They were yet unbelievers, but mark the magnanimity of that great soul who would not even reproach them for their evil deeds, who let them go even without taking a pledge from them for the future. Here was a practical proof of that laudable precept, *Love thine enemy*. Not only was Mecca conquered, but with it were conquered also the hearts of the bitterest foes of Islām. They now saw with their own eyes how the combined forces of opposition offered by the whole country had proved an utter failure against the mighty truth which came from the lips of a man who had stood alone in the midst of all opposition. The righteousness of the cause was now only too clear to them and men and women came forward spontaneously to embrace the faith. There was not a single instance of conversion by force.

Those that still adhered to the old religion were treated in the same spirit of friendliness as the members of the brotherhood. Even a hostile critic has to admit:

> Although the city had cheerfully accepted his authority, all its inhabitants had not yet embraced the new religion nor formally acknowledged his prophetical claim. Perhaps he intended to follow the course he had pursued at Medina and leave the conversion of the people to be gradually accomplished without compulsion.[23]

The fall of Mecca was a signal to the whole of Arabia. In fact, the Quraish were generally at the bottom of all organized opposition. With the sole exception of the battle of Ḥunain, which had to be undertaken against the Hawāzin immediately after the conquest of Mecca, regular warfare between the Muslims and the non-Muslims,

---

22. 12:92   23. Sir William Muir

in the whole of Arabia now came to an end, and even at Ḥunain, the unbelieving Meccans fought on the side of the Muslims.

Islām was now free from trouble within, but the Christian power on the north viewed its strength with a jealous eye, and persistent news as to preparations of the Roman Empire to attack Arabia could not be ignored. Accordingly, an expedition of 30,000 men was led by the Prophet personally to the northern frontier in the ninth year of the flight. When he reached Tabūk, however, he found that his march had a restraining effect on the enemy, and there being no hostile force in the field, the Prophet returned without either attacking the Romans or declaring war against them. In fact, the Prophet always observed the Quranic injunction to fight only with those who took up the sword first to fight against the Muslims.

After the return from Tabūk, peace was apparently established in the peninsula, but the Islāmic territory was infested with hordes of marauders belonging to the tribes that had entered into agreement with the Muslim state, but had little respect for their treaties: "Those with whom thou makest an agreement, then they break their agreement every time and they have no regard for their obligations."[24] These people had become a menace to the security of life and property, and accordingly, towards the end of the ninth year of the Hijra, the Prophet sent 'Ali to make an important declaration of immunity regarding such agreements at the annual pilgrimage at Mecca. This declaration is contained in the opening verses of the chapter entitled *The Immunity*: "This is a declaration of immunity by Allāh and His Messenger towards those of the idolaters with whom you made an agreement"[25]

By idolaters were meant the idolaters spoken of in the previous chapter, already referred to, "those with whom Thou makest an agreement then they break their agreement every time." This is made clear in the next few verses by making an exception in favour of those who had not violated their treaties:

---

24. 8:56   25. 9:1

> Except those of the idolaters with whom you made an agreement then they have not failed you in anything and have not aided any one against you so fulfil their agreement to the end of their term, for Allāh loves those who have regard for their obligations.[26]

And again:

> How can there be an agreement for the idolaters with Allāh and His Messenger, except those with whom you made an agreement at the Sacred Mosque; so as long as they are true to you be true to them, for Allāh loves those who have regard for their obligations. How can it be! For if they prevail against you, they will not pay regard in your case to ties of relationship, nor those of their covenant; they please you with their mouths while their hearts do not consent and most of them are transgressors ... They do not pay regard to ties of relationship nor those of covenant in the case of a believer, and these are they who exceed the limits.[27]

The idolaters concerned met 'Ali with the retort: "O 'Ali! Deliver this message to thy cousin (i.e. the Prophet) that we have thrown the agreements behind our backs and there is no agreement between him and us except smiting with spears and striking with swords." The result of the Prophet's firm attitude was that such tribes surrendered, and a settled condition of peace prevailed throughout the peninsula.

This declaration of immunity towards the violaters is sometimes misunderstood as meaning an abrogation of the conditions of war laid down at the beginning: "Fight with those who fight with you and do not exceed this limit." As a matter of fact, the condition laid down remained effective to the end. The Prophet's return from Tabūk without attacking either the Roman territory or the territory of any other tribe is a clear evidence of this. And even after the declaration of immunity, the Muslims were required to fight with those who attacked them first:

---

26. 9:4   27. 9:7-10

> What! Will you not fight a people who broke their oaths and aimed at the expulsion of the Messenger and attacked you first?[28]

Deputations which had already started coming to the Prophet in the ninth year of the Flight to learn the truth about Islām now became more abundant. People came from different corners from all over Arabia and embraced Islām of their own free will. As soon as peace was established, Islām spread by leaps and bounds, and the tenth year of the Flight witnessed the conversion of the whole of Arabia to Islām, including some Christian tribes. It was not only a conversion in the sense that idolatry was given up for the purest monotheism from one end of the vast peninsula to the other; it was a reformation in all spheres of life. The whole course of life of an entire nation was changed - ignorance, superstition and barbarism giving place to the spread of knowledge and to a rational outlook in all aspects of life.

At the end of the tenth year of the Hijra, the Prophet set out to perform the pilgrimage to Mecca. As the whole of Arabia was now Muslim, there was not a single idolater in the huge concourse of 124,000 pilgrims assembled at Mecca from all corners of the country. The very spot where the Prophet was only twenty years ago a rejected person, to whose word no one was willing to lend his ear, was now the scene of marvellous devotion to him. To whichever side he turned his eye, he saw hosts of devoted friends who recognized him both as their temporal as well as their spiritual head. An inspiring manifestation of Divine power to him as well as to those who had assembled there.

It was here on the ninth day of Dhul Hijja, the day of the assembling of the pilgrims at Mount 'Arafat, that he received a revelation from on High which sent a thrill of joy through the vast gathering:

---

28. 9:13

This day have I perfected your religion for you and completed My favour to you and chosen for you al-Islām as a religion.[29]

Obviously the Prophet perceived that the message of the perfection of religion meant his approaching end. Here he delivered the following sermon - Islām's sermon on the Mount - to the whole of Arabia through representatives of tribes coming from every quarter:

O people! Lend an attentive ear to my words, for I know not whether I shall ever hereafter have the opportunity to meet you here. ... I apprise you that your lives, your properties and your honour must be as sacred to one another as this sacred day in this sacred month in this sacred town. Let those present take this message to those absent. You are about to meet your Lord Who will call you to account for your deeds ...

O people! This day Satan has despaired of re-establishing his power in this land of yours. But should you obey him even in what may seem to you a trifling matter, it will be a source of pleasure for him. So you must beware of him in the matter of your faith.

O my people! You have certain rights over your wives and so have your wives over you ... They are the trust of Allāh in your hands. So you must treat them with all kindness ... And as regards your slaves, see that you give them to eat of what you yourselves eat and clothe them with what you clothe yourselves.

O people! Listen to what I say and take it to heart. You must know that every Muslim is the brother of another Muslim. You are all equal, and members of one brotherhood. It is forbidden to any of you to take from his brother save what he should willingly give. Do not do injustice to your people.

---

29. 5:3

Then the Prophet cried at the top of his voice:

O Allāh! I have delivered Thy message,

and the valley resounded with the words:

Aye! That thou hast.

This is known as the Prophet's Farewell pilgrimage. A little while after his return to Medina, he fell ill. At first he went to the mosque to lead the prayers even during his illness, but later on he became too weak and appointed Abū Bakr to lead the prayers. After about twelve days' illness, on the 12th of Rabī'I on a Monday in the 11th year of the Flight, at the age of sixty-three, he commended his soul to his Maker, His last words being:

Blessed companionship on High.

The most outstanding characteristic of the life of the Prophet is the amazing success which he achieved. The transformation wrought within the short space of less than a quarter of a century is in fact unparalleled in the history of the world. There is not a single reformer who brought about such an entire change in the lives of a whole nation inhabiting such a vast country. None, in fact, found his people at such a depth of degradation as the Prophet found the Arabs, and no one raised them materially, morally and spiritually to the height to which he raised them. So deep-rooted was their idolatry, so powerful the bonds of their superstitions and their usages that the propagandic efforts of the Jews and the Christians, carried on for hundreds of years one after the other, with the material power of the kingdoms at their back, could not bring about the least change in their condition. The indigenous Arab movement of the Hanīfs proved an even greater failure. All these attempts at reform left the Arabs as a nation as ignorant of the principles of religion and morality as they ever were. Twenty-three years' work of the Prophet, however, quite metamorphosed them. Worship of idols and of all objects other than God, whether in heaven or on earth, was now considered to be a disgrace to humanity. No trace of an idol was left throughout the whole of Arabia. The whole nation awakened to a sense of the true dignity of manhood and realized the folly of falling prostrate before things which man was made to rule and before powers which he was required to conquer. Superstition gave place to a rational religion. The Arab was not only cleansed of deep-rooted vice and bare-faced immorality; he was further inspired with a burning desire for the best and noblest deeds in the service of, no country and nation, but, what is far higher than that, humanity. Old customs which involved injustice to the weak and the oppressed were all swept away, as if by a magician's wand, and just and reasonable laws took their place. Drunkenness, to which Arabia was addicted from time immemorial, disappeared so entirely that the very goblets and vessels which were used for drinking and keeping wine could no more be found. Gambling was quite unknown, and the loose relations of the sexes gave place to the highest regard for chastity. The Arab who prided himself on ignorance became the lover of knowledge, drinking deep at every fountain of learning to which he could get access. And greatest of all, from an Arabia, the various elements of which were so constantly at war with each other that the whole country was about to perish, was indeed on the "brink of a pit of fire,"[30] as the Holy Quran so tersely puts it - from these jarring and warring elements, the Prophet welded together a nation, a united nation full of life and vigour, before whose onward march the greatest kingdoms of the world crumbled as if they were but toys before the reality of the new faith. No man ever breathed such a new life on such a wide scale - a life affecting all branches of human activity; a transformation of the individual, of the family, of the society, of the nation, of the country; an awakening, material as well as moral, intellectual as well as spiritual. Here are a few testimonies from non-Muslim writers:

> The prospects of Arabia before Muḥammad were as unfavourable to religious reform as they were to political union or national regeneration. The foundation of Arab faith was a deep-rooted idolatry which for centuries, had stood proof, with no palpable symptom of decay, against every attempt at evangelization from Egypt and Syria.[31]

---

30. 3:103   31. Sir William Muir

During the youth of Muḥammad, the aspect of the Peninsula was strongly conservative; perhaps never at any previous time was reform more hopeless.[32]

Causes are sometime conjured up to account for results produced by an agent apparently inadequate to effect them. Muḥammad arose, and forthwith the Arabs were aroused to a new and spiritual faith; hence the conclusion that Arabia was fermenting for the change, and prepared to adopt it. To us calmly reviewing the past, pre-Islāmite history belies the assumption.[33]

From time beyond memory Mecca and the whole Peninsula had been steeped in spiritual torpor. The slight and transient influences of Judaism, Christianity, or philosophical enquiry upon the Arab mind had been but as the ruffling here and there of the surface of a quiet lake; all remained still and motionless below. The people were sunk in superstition, cruelty and vice ... Their religion was a gross idolatry; and their faith, the dark superstitious dread of unseen things ... Thirteen years before the Hijra, Mecca lay lifeless in this debased state. What a change had these thirteen years now produced ... Jewish truth had long sounded in the ears of the men of Medina; but it was not until they heard the spirit-stirring strains of the Arabian Prophet that they too awoke from their slumber, and sprang suddenly into a new and earnest life.[34]

And yet we may truly say that no history can boast events that strike the imagination in a more lively manner or can be more surprising in themselves, than those we meet with in the life of the first Mussalmans; whether we consider the Great Chief, or his ministers, the most illustrious of men; or whether we take an account of the manners of the several countries he conquered; or observe the courage, virtue and

---

32. Sir William Muir   33. *Ibid.*   34. *Ibid.*

sentiments that equally prevailed among his generals and soldiers.[35]

A more disunited people it would be hard to find, till, suddenly, the miracle took place. A man arose who, by his personality and by his claim to direct Divine guidance, actually brought about the impossible, namely, the union of all these warring factions.[36]

Never has a people been led more rapidly to civilization, such as it was, than were the Arabs through Islām.[37]

Such then, very briefly, was the condition of the Arabs, social and religious, when, to use an expression of Voltaire, ... 'the turn of Arabia came'; when the hour had already struck for the most complete, the most sudden and the most extraordinary revolution that had ever come over any nation upon earth.[38]

Of all the religious personalities of the world, Muḥammad was the most successful.[39]

The man who brought about the most thorough transformation of a nation within twenty years; who, alone and unaided, swept away vice and immorality from a whole country where the most strenuous efforts of a powerful missionary nation had hopelessly failed; who by his personal example purified the lives of vast numbers of humanity; could such a man himself be in the grip of sin? An impure man could not consistently preach virtue; how could he take others by the hand, and free them from the bondage of sin, and inspire his very soldiers and generals with sentiments of virtue? Could a man who himself groped in the dark lead others to light? Yet the Prophet - this great deliverer of humanity from the bondage of sin - is called

---

35. *Life of Muhammad*, by Count of Boulainvilliers
36. *Ins and Outs of Mespot.*
37. *New Researches*, by Hirschfeld
38. Bosworth Smith
39. *Encyclopaedia Britannica*, 11th edition, Art. "Koran."

sinful because at a certain stage in his life he had more wives than one.

Whatever may be the views on polygamy of the modern world, there is not the least doubt that plurality of wives is met with in the lives of the great religious personages who by a consensus of opinion led lives of transcendent purity. Abraham, who is held in reverence by more than half the world up to this day, had more wives than one. Similar was the cases with Jacob, Moses and David among the Israelites, and with some of the famous revered Hindus. Yet it is true that these great sages were not led to a polygamous life by sensual desires. Purity in all respects is the outstanding characteristic of their lives, and this fact alone is sufficient to condemn the attempt to defame them on the basis of their resorting to polygamy. What was their object in doing so, it is difficult to say at the present day, as their histories are generally enveloped in darkness, but as the life of the Prophet can be read in the full light of history, we will take his case in detail.

The life of the Prophet may be divided into four periods so far as his domestic life is concerned. Up to twenty-five he led a celibate life; from twenty-five to fifty-four he lived in a married state with one wife; from fifty-four to sixty he contracted several marriages; and lastly, from sixty till his death he did not contract any new marriage. The most important period to determine whether the Prophet was a slave to his passions is the period of celibacy. If he had not been a complete master of his passions, he could not have led an exceptionally chaste and pure life, which won him the title of *al-Amīn*, to the age of twenty-five in a hot country like Arabia where development must necessarily take place early and passions are generally stronger. His worst enemies could not point to a single blot on his character when challenged later. According to Muir, all authorities agree "in ascribing to the youth of Muḥammad a modesty of deportment and purity of manners rare among the people of Mecca." Now, youth is the time when passions run riot, and the man who is able to control his passions in youth, and that in celibacy, cannot, possibly, be conceived as falling a prey to lust in his old age. Thus the first period of his life, his celibacy up to twenty-five years of age, is conclusive proof that he could never fall a prey to his passions. It should be noted in this connection that in Arab society at the time there was no moral sanction against an immoral life, so that it cannot be said that he was kept back from an evil course by the moral force of society. Profligacy, on the other hand, was the order of the day; and it was among people who prided themselves on loose sexual relations that the Prophet led a life of transcendent purity, and therefore all the more credit is due to his purity of character.

Take now the next period, the period of a monogamous married life. When twenty-five years of age, Muḥammad married a widow, Khadīja, fifteen years his senior, and led a life of the utmost devotion with her till she died, when he was fifty years of age. Polygamy was the rule in Arabia at the time; and the wife had no cause of complaint, nor did she ever grumble, if the husband brought in a second or third wife. The Prophet belonged to the noblest family of the Quraish and his marriage with Khadīja had enriched him; and if he had chosen to marry another wife, it would have been quite easy for him. But he led a monogamous life of the utmost devotion to his wife during all that time. When Khadīja died, he married a very elderly lady, Sauda, whose only recommendation for the honour was that she was the widow of a faithful companion of his who had to flee to Abyssinia from the persecution of the Quraish. The main part of his life, from twenty-five to fifty-four, was thus an example for his followers that monogamy was the rule in married life.

Now comes the third period. Of all his wives 'Ā'isha was the only one whom he married as a virgin. Her father, Abū Bakr, the closest friend of the Prophet, had offered her to him when he suffered the great bereavement of losing both his wife and his uncle Abū Ṭālib. The girl was one possessing exceptional qualities, and both Abū Bakr and the Prophet saw in her the great woman of the future who was best suited to perform the duties of the wife of a teacher who was to be a perfect exemplar for mankind. So the Prophet accepted her; but apparently she had not yet reached the age of puberty,[40] and her marriage was consummated towards the close of the second year of the Flight.

In the second year of the Flight began the series of battles with the Quraish and the other Arab tribes, which appreciably reduced the number of males, the bread-winners of the family. These battles continued up to the eighth year of the Flight, and it was during this time that the Prophet contracted all the marriages which appear objectionable to the modern mind, but which neither friend nor foe looked upon with disapprobation at the time. A Christian writer says:

> It would be remembered, however, that most of Muhammad's marriages may be explained at least as much by his pity for the forlorn condition of the persons concerned, as by other motives. They were almost all of them widows who were not remarkable either for their beauty or their wealth, but quite the reverse.[41]

---

40. A great misconception prevails as to the age at which 'Ā'isha was taken in marriage by the Prophet. Ibn Sa'd has stated in the *Tabaqāt* that when Abū Bakr was approached on behalf of the Holy Prophet, he replied that the girl had already been betrothed to Jubair, and that he would have to settle the matter first with him. This shows that 'Ā'isha must have been approaching majority at the time. Again, the *Isāba*, speaking on the Prophet's daughter Fatima, says that she was born five years before the Call and was about five years older than 'Ā'isha. This shows that 'Ā'isha must have been about ten years at the time of her betrothal to the Prophet, and not six years as she is generally supposed to be. This is further borne out by the fact that 'Ā'isha herself is reported to have stated that when the chapter entitled "The Moon" (fifty-fourth chapter) was revealed, she was a girl playing about and remembered certain verses then revealed. Now the fifty-fourth chapter was undoubtedly revealed before the sixth year of the Call. All these considerations point to but one conclusion, viz., that 'Ā'isha could not have been less than ten years of age at the time of her *nikāh*, which was virtually only a betrothal. And there is one report in the *Tabaqāt* that 'Ā'isha was nine years of age at the time of *nikāh*. Again it is a fact admitted on all hands that the *nikāh* of 'Ā'isha took place in the tenth year of the Call in the month of Shawwāl, while there is also preponderance of evidence as to the consummation of her marriage taking place in the second year of Hijra in the same month, which shows that full five years had elapsed between the *nikāh* and the consummation. Hence there is not the least doubt that 'Ā'isha was at least nine or ten years of age at the time of betrothal, and fourteen or fifteen years at the time of marriage.
41. Bosworth Smith

Let us look the facts straight in the face. The Prophet had now in his house a young and beautiful wife in 'Ā'isha. None of the other wives whom he married later compared with her either in youth or beauty. Surely then it was not attraction for beauty that led to these marriages. We have already seen that from his youth till his old age the Prophet remained a complete master of his passions. The man who could live in celibacy up to twenty-five and still have the reputation of a spotless character, who up to fifty-four lived with a single wife and this notwithstanding the fact that polygamy was more the rule than the exception at the time and that a polygamous connection was not in the least objectionable — such a man could not be said to have changed all of a sudden after fifty-five when old age generally soothes the passions even of those who cannot control their passions in youth. No other motive than compassion for the ladies who were given this honour can be attached to these marriages. If there had been any less honourable motive, his choice would have fallen on others than widows, and under the Arab custom a man in his position could have plenty of youthful virgins.

I have said that a change for the worse could not come over a man who had led an undoubtedly spotless life until he reached fifty-five. If the beauty of women could not excite his passions in youth and lead him away from the path of rectitude, how could it lead him away in old age? And what were the circumstances in which he lived at Medina during these years? It was not a life of ease and luxury that he was leading at the time; it was a life of hardness, because it was at this very time that he had to carry on a life-and-death struggle with the enemies of Islām. Huge armies came to crush him and the small band of Muslims at Medina. The whole of Arabia was aflame against him. He was not secure for a minute. Battles had to be fought in quick succession. Expeditions had to be arranged and sent. "Prophet of God! We are tired of being in arms day and night," his companions would say to him; and he had to console them by telling them that the time would come when a traveller would be able to go from one end of the country to the other without having any arms. The Jews and the Christians were his enemies along with the idolaters. His best friends were falling sometimes in battle and sometimes by treachery. Is it possible for a man to lead a life of ease and luxury under such circumstances? Even if a man had the mind to lead a life of self-indulgence, which the Prophet according to all available evidence had not, this was not the opportune time for it. In such circumstances of warfare, with enemies within Medina and enemies all around it, with the number of Muslims being insignificantly small in comparison with the enemy, with news of assaults by overwhelming numbers on all sides, even a profligate's life would be changed, to say nothing of a man of avowed purity of character, which no temptation could shake, turning into a profligate.

If the Prophet's days during this period were passed so strenuously, how did he pass the nights? He had a number of lawful wives, but he did not spend his nights in enjoyment with them. There is the clearest evidence on record in the Holy Quran as well as the Hadīth that he passed half, and sometimes even two-thirds, of the night in prayers and in reciting the Holy Quran while standing in prayer. He would stand so long that his feet would get swollen. Could such a man be said to be taking wives for self-indulgence when the minutest details of his life as available to us show conclusively that it was a strenuous life furthest away from indulgence of any kind?

Let us now consider another point. Was any change really witnessed in the latter part of his life when he became the ruler of a state? "In the shepherd of the desert, in the Syrian trader, in the solitary of Mount Hira, in the reformer in the minority of one, in the exile of Medina, in the acknowledged conqueror, in the equal of the Persian Chosroes and the Greek Heraclius, we can still trace a substantial unity. I doubt whether any other man, whose external conditions changed so much, ever himself changed less to meet them: the accidents are changed, the essence seems to me to be the same in all."[42]

From the cradle to the grave the Prophet passed through a diversity of circumstances — diversity which can hardly be met with

---

42. Bosworth Smith

in the life of a single man. Orphanhood is the extreme of helplessness, while kingship is the height of power. From being an orphan he climbed to the summit of royal glory, but that did not bring about the slightest change in his way of living. He lived on exactly the same kind of humble food, wore the same simple dress, and in all particulars led the same simple life as he led in the state of orphanhood. It is hard to give up the kingly throne and lead the life of a hermit, but it is harder still that one should wield the royal sceptre yet at the same time lead a hermit's life, that one should possess power and wealth yet spend it solely to promote the welfare of others, that one should ever have the most alluring attractions before one's eyes yet should never for one moment be captivated by them. When the Prophet actually became the ruler of a state, the furniture of his house was composed of a coarse matting of palm leaves for his bed and an earthen jug for water. Some nights he would go without food. For days no fire would be lighted in his house to prepare food, the whole family living on mere dates. There was no lack of means to live a life of ease and comfort. The public treasury was at his disposal. The well-to-do among his followers, who did not shrink from sacrificing their lives for his sake, would have been only too glad to provide him with every comfort of life, should he choose to avail himself of it. But worldly things carried little weight in his estimation. No mundane craving could ever prevail over him, neither in times of indigence nor of plenty. Just as he spurned wealth, power and beauty which the Quraish offered him when he was yet in a state of utmost helplessness, so did he remain indifferent to them when God granted him all these things out of His grace.

Not only did he himself live the simple life of a labourer, but he did not even allow wealth to have any attraction for his wives. Shortly after their immigration into Medina, the condition of the Muslims had changed, and they carried on a prosperous trade. Their conquests, later on, went further to add to the comforts of life which the Muslims enjoyed. A quite human desire crept into the hearts of the Prophet's wives that, like other Muslim families, they too should avail themselves of their share of comforts. Accordingly, they approached the Prophet in a body to prevail upon him to allow them their legitimate share of worldly comforts. Thereupon came the Divine injunction:

> O Prophet! Say to thy wives, If you desire this world's life and its adornment, come, I will give you a provision and allow you to depart a goodly departing. And if you desire Allāh and His Messenger and the latter abode, then surely Allāh has prepared for the doers of good among you a mighty reward.[43]

Thus they were offered two alternatives. They might either have worldly finery, or remain in the Prophet's household. Should they decide to have the former, they would have plenty of what they wanted, but would forthwith forfeit the honour of being the Prophet's wives. Is this the reply of a sensual man? Such a man would have done everything to satisfy the whims of the objects of his affection. Nay, he would himself have desired that his wives should wear the most beautiful dress and live in comfort. No doubt the Prophet cherished great love for his wives. He had immense regard for the rights of women and was the champion of their cause. But when his wives came to him with what was apparently a quite legitimate demand to have more finery and ornaments, they were coldly told that if they would have these things they were not fit to live in the Prophet's house. This shows beyond a shadow of doubt how free the Prophet's mind was of all base and sensual thoughts. He was prepared to divorce all his wives rather than yield to what he regarded as unworthy of his wives - an inclination towards worldly things. It shows conclusively that the object of his marriages was anything but self-indulgence.

Let us consider once more the historical facts which led the Prophet to take a number of wives within the short space of five years from the third year of Hijra to the seventh, while before that he passed nearly thirty years of his life in a monogamous state. This period coincides exactly with the period during which incessant war

---

43. 33:28, 29

was carried on between the Muslims and the non-Muslims. The circle of Muslim brotherhood was at the time very narrow. The perpetual state of war created disparity between the male and the female elements of society. Husbands having fallen on the field of battle, their widows had to be provided for. But bread and butter was not the only provision needed in such cases. Sex-inclination is implanted in human nature, and the statesman who neglects the sex requirements leads society to moral corruption, ending ultimately in the ruin of the whole nation. A reformer with whom morals were all in all could not content himself with making provison merely for the maintenance of the widows. The Prophet was anxious for their chastity to a far greater extent than their physical needs. It became therefore necessary to allow polygamy. This is the reason that he himself took so many women for his wives during the period when war was raging. Nearly all his wives were widows. If self-indulgence were the motive, the choice would not have fallen on widows. It would have been an enviable privilege for any Muslim to be the father-in-law of the Prophet. But the object was a noble one - the protection of the widows of his friends. In polygamy alone lay the safety of the Muslim society.

We now come to the fourth period. With the conquest of Mecca in 8 A.H., internal warfare came practically to an end. Disturbances there were, but, on the whole, peace had been established in the country and normal conditions were restored. From the eighth year of the Flight to the end of his life we again find that the Prophet did not contract any new marriage. What is the evidence of the facts then? The Prophet added to the number of his wives only during the time that he had to live in a state of warfare, when the number of males was reduced and many women would have been left without protection and without a home if the difficulty had not been solved by permitting a limited polygamy. Before the Prophet had to enter on a defensive war, he lived in the company of a single wife, and when war ended, he contracted no new marriage. This sets all doubts at rest as to the motive of the Prophet. In all the marriages which he contracted during the war, there was some ulterior moral end in view. There arose situations in his life under which he could not consistently, with the moral and religious mission of his life, help taking more wives than one. In that, he only showed compassion to the weaker sex.

Living in a country in which polygamy was the rule, the Prophet had no liking for polygamy. He passed the prime of his life, up to fifty-four years of age, as the husband of a single wife, thus showing that the union of one man and one woman was the rule under normal conditions. But when abnormal conditions arose, he did not, like a sentimentalist, shirk his duty. He saw that the chastity of woman was at stake if polygamy was not allowed, and for the sake of a higher interest he permitted polygamy as an exception to meet exceptional circumstances. Exactly thus he had to resort to war, though by disposition he was averse to it. Full forty years before the Call, he had been living in a land where the sword was wielded as freely as a stick elsewhere, where fighting and feuds were the order of the day, where men would fly at each other's throats like wild animals, where there was no chance of survival for one who could not use the sword, yet not once during these forty years did he deal a blow at an enemy. The same was the case with him for fourteen years after the Call.

That he was peace-loving by nature is shown by the clear injunctions relating to peace in the Holy Quran: "And if they incline to peace, do thou also incline to it and trust in Allāh ... And if they intend to deceive thee, than surely Allāh is sufficient for thee."[44]

The Prophet's acceptance of the truce of Ḥudaibiya, though its conditions were humiliting for the Muslims, who were ready to lay down their lives one and all rather than accept those terms, is also a clear proof of his peace-loving nature. But when duty called him to take the field to save his community, he did not hesitate to take up the sword against an overwhelming majority. He acted as a sagacious general in all fields of battle and behaved like a brave soldier when opportunity demanded. He knew how to disperse an enemy in time before it had gained sufficient strength to deal a severe blow at the Muslims. And once, in the battle of Ḥunain, when his army was in

---

44. 8:61, 62

flight owing to the severe onslaught of the enemy's archers, he was all alone advancing towards the enemy forces, till his soldiers rallied round him. By disposition he had no inclination for war, yet circumstances arose which dragged him into the field of battle, and he then displayed the wisdom of a general and the bravery of a soldier. So by disposition he was not inclined to polygamy, living a celibate life of unexampled purity up to twenty-five years of age and a married life of a monogamous husband up to fifty-four, but when duty called him to take more women under his shelter, he answered the call of duty.

Brief as this treatment of the Prophet's life is, it would be incomplete without a few words as to his manners and morals. When his wife, 'Ā'isha, the most privy to his secrets, was questioned about his morals, her reply was, "His morals are the Quran." In other words, the highest morals that were depicted in the Holy Quran were possessed by him.

Simplicity and sincerity are the keynotes of the Prophet's character. He would do all sorts of things with his own hands. He would milk his own goats, patch his own clothes and mend his own shoes. In person would he dust the house, and he would tie his camel and look after it personally. No work was too low for him. He worked like a labourer in the construction of the mosque, and again in digging a ditch round Medina. In person would he do shopping, not only for his own household, but also for his neighbours or for helpless women. He never despised any work, however humble, notwithstanding the dignity of his position as Prophet and King. He thus demonstrated through personal example that man's calling does not really determine his nobleness or his meanness.

His actions and movements were characterized by homely simplicity. He did not like his companions to stand up on his arrival. Once he forbade them, saying, "Do not stand up for me as do the non-Arabs;" and added that he was a humble creature of God, eating as others eat and sitting as others sit. When a certain man wanted to kiss his hand, he withdrew it remarking that that was the behaviour of the non-Arabs towards their kings. Even if a slave sent him an invitation he accepted it. He would take his meals in the company of all classes of people, even of slaves. When seated among people, there was nothing about him to make him conspicuous.

The Prophet had a deep love for his friends. While shaking hands with them, he would never be the first to withdraw his hand. He met everybody with a smiling face. A report from Jarīr ibn 'Abdullāh says that he never saw the Prophet but with a smile on his face. He would talk freely, never putting on artificial reserve to give himself an air of superiority. He would take up children in arms and nurse them. He disliked backbiting and forbade his visitors to talk ill of any of his friends. He would ever take the lead in greeting his friends and shaking hands with them.

The Prophet's generosity even towards his enemies stands unique in the annals of the world. 'Abdullāh ibn Ubayy, the head of the hypocrites, was a sworn enemy of Islām, and his days and nights were spent in plotting mischief against the Muslims. Yet at his death, the Prophet prayed to the Lord to forgive him and even granted his own shirt to enshroud his body. The Meccans, who had all along subjected him and his friends to the most barbarous tortures, were not only awarded a general amnesty but were let off even without a reproof. Twenty long years of persecutions and warfare were absolutely forgiven and forgotten. "The magnanimity with which Muḥammad treated a people who had so long hated and rejected him is worthy of all admiration," says Muir. The fact is that no other example is met with in history of such magnanimous forgiveness of inveterate enemies, who had shed innocent blood, who had shown no pity for helpless men, women and children, who had exerted themselves to their utmost to kill the Prophet and to annihilate the Muslims. The prisoners of war were almost always set free even without demanding a ransom. It was only in the case of the prisoners of Badr that ransom was demanded; after that, hundreds of prisoners and in one case, in the battle with Hawāzin, as many as six thousand, were released without taking a single piece of ransom. At the battle of Uḥud, when he was wounded and fell down, a comrade asked him to curse his persecutors. His reply was: "I have not been sent to curse but as an inviter to good and mercy. O Lord! guide my people, for they know not." Once a Bedouin pulled him and threw his wrap round his neck. When asked why he should not be repaid in the same coin, he pleaded that he (the Prophet) never returned evil for evil.

In the administration of justice, the Prophet was scrupulously even-handed. Muslims and non-Muslims, friend and foe, were all alike in his eyes. Even before the Call, his impartiality, his honesty and integrity were of household fame, and people would bring their disputes to him to settle. At Medina, the Jews and idolaters both accepted him as the arbitrator in all their disputes. Notwithstanding the deep-rooted malice of the Jews against Islām, when a case between a Jew and a Muslim once came up before him, he decreed in favour of the Jew, regardless of the fact that the Muslim, nay, even perhaps the whole of his tribe, might thereby be alienated. In his dealings with his worst enemies he was always true to the Quranic injunction which says: "Let not hatred of a people incite you not to act equitably; act equitably, that is nearer to piety."[45] On his death-bed, immediately before he breathed his last, he had it publicly announced: "If I owe anything to anybody, it may be claimed; if I have offended anybody, he may have his revenge."

In his dealings with others he never placed himself on a higher pedestal. Once while he held the position of a king at Medina, a Jew whom he owed some money came up to him and began to abuse him. 'Umar was enraged, but the Prophet rebuked him, saying: "It would have been meet for thee to have advised both of us - me, the debtor to repay the debt with gratitude, and him, the creditor, to demand it in a more becoming manner." And he paid the Jew more than his due. On another occasion when he was out in the wood with his friends, the time for preparation of food came. Everybody was allotted a piece of work, he himself going out to pick up fuel. Spiritual and temporal overlord though he was, he would yet do his share of work like an ordinary man. In his treatment of his servants, he observed the same principle of equality. A report from Anas says that during the ten years that he was in the Prophet's service at Medina, where he ultimately became the master of the whole of

---

45. 5:8

Arabia, he was not once scolded by him. He never kept anybody in slavery. As soon as he got a slave, he set him free.

In charity the Prophet was simply unapproached. He never gave a flat refusal to a beggar. He would feed the hungry, himself going without food. He never kept any money in his possession. While on his death-bed, he sent for whatever there was in his house and distributed it among the poor. Even for the dumb creatures of God his heart overflowed with mercy. He spoke of one who drew water from a well to quench the thirst of a dog as having earned paradise with this act of kindness. He spoke of a deceased woman that she was undergoing punishment because she would tie up her cat and keep it hungry. From his earliest days he had a deep sympathy for widows and orphans, the poor and the helpless. He would ever stand by the oppressed. He vindicated the rights of women over men, of slaves over their masters, of the ruled over the rulers, and of the subjects over the king. Negro slaves were accorded the same position of honour as the Quraish leaders. He was the champion of the oppressed and the ill-treated ones. He was very fond of children, and while walking along he would pat and stroke those whom he met on the way. Without fail would he visit the sick to enquire after their health and console them. He would also accompany a funeral.

Humble and meek in the highest degree, he had yet the courage of the bravest of men. Never for a moment did he harbour fear of his enemies. Even when plots to take his life were being hatched in Mecca, he moved about fearlessly day and night. He told all his companions to emigrate from Mecca, himself remaining almost alone among infuriated enemies. With his pursuers at the mouth of the cave in which he had hidden himself, he could yet console his companion, saying, "Allāh is with us." On the field of Uḥud when the whole of his army fell into a trap, he shouted aloud, regardless of all danger to his own person, to rally the confused soldiers. In the battle of Ḥunain when the Muslim rank and file took to flight, he advanced alone towards the enemy, calling aloud, "I am the Prophet." When one night a raid was suspected, he was the first to reconnoitre the outskirts of Medina, riding his horse without saddling it. On a certain journey, while resting under a tree all alone, an enemy came upon him, and unsheathing his sword shouted out: "Who can save thee now from my hands?" Calmly the Prophet replied, "Allāh." And the next moment the same sword was in the Prophet's hand who put to his enemy the same question, on which he assumed a tone of abject humility, and the Prophet let him go.

The Prophet's integrity and sincerity were of universal fame throughout Arabia. His worst enemies had often to confess that he had never told a lie. When he once pledged his word, he kept it under the most trying conditions and even at a heavy cost. He faithfully observed the truce made at Ḥudaibiya, though he had to refuse shelter to Muslims escaping from the persecutions of the Meccans. His biographers are all at one in their admiration of his unflinching fortitude and unswerving steadfastness. Despair and despondency were unknown to him. Hemmed in as he was on all sides by a gloomy prospect and severe opposition, his faith in the ultimate triumph of the truth was never for one moment shaken.

Chapter 2
Faith in God

What was the secret of the success of "The most successful of all the religious personalities of the world?" What was the thought upon which was based "the most complete, the most sudden and the most extraordinary revolution that had ever come over any nation upon earth?" How were men's minds prepared for this unparalleled and thorough transformation? How was "a new and earnest life" breathed into a people that were sunk deep in "superstition, cruelty and vice?" How was the "impossible" task performed of uniting into one whole the warring factions that were bent upon destroying each other? What was the root remedy applied to the ills of humanity?

The secret of the Prophet's success, a success admittedly unparalleled to this day, lay in his strong faith in God. He had a deep conviction that God had a plan for the uplift of man, to bring to perfection not one nation or one people but the whole world, and that no power in the world could frustrate the Divine purpose. When the first message came to him that he was commissioned to save a fallen humanity, he actually trembled. From his solitude in the cave of Ḥirā', he came home to his wife trembling, and asked her to wrap him up. It was the magnitude of the task which made him shake. But he set to work immediately. He was at first ridiculed, called an idle visionary, and treated with contempt as unworthy of serious attention. But as he gained ground, opposition started in real earnest, and he and his followers were subjected to the severest persecutions. Cruel tortures were inflicted on them, some of them had to suffer torture even to death. Unbaffled he advised his followers to betake themselves to Abyssinia where a Christian monarch ruled. "There is a land," he said, "where no one is wronged - a land of justice. Stay there until it shall please Allāh to open for you a way out of these difficulties."

He had a deep conviction that difficulties would disappear. His followers thus reached a place of security but he himself stuck to his post, alone and undaunted. He was threatened with murder, and even Abū Ṭālib, his uncle and his sole support, told him that he could no more withstand the united opposition of the Quraish. "Do not charge me," he said to the Prophet, "with a responsibility too heavy for me." But the Prophet stood adamant. "Should they place the sun O uncle!" he said, "in my right hand and the moon in my left, in order to make me renounce this mission, I should not do it. I shall never give it up until it shall please Allāh to make it triumph or I perish in the attempt." Failing in the attempt to persuade Abū Ṭālib to hand over the Prophet to them, they approached him directly: "If your ambition is to possess wealth, we will amass for you as much of it as you wish; if you aspire to win honour, we are prepared to swear allegiance to you as our overlord and king; if you have a fancy for beauty, we offer you the hand of the finest maiden of your own choice." The temptations were nigh irresistible. From a destitute, helpless and persecuted man to a mighty potentate rolling in wealth and with beauty by his side was a big lift. But he replied: "I want neither riches nor political power. I have been commissioned by Allāh as a warner to mankind, and I deliver His message to you. Should you accept it, you shall have felicity in this life as well as in the life to come; should you reject the word of Allāh, surely Allāh will decide between you and me."

Referring to this it is said in one of the early revelations:

> And they had indeed purposed to turn thee away from that which We have revealed to thee that thou shouldst forge against Us other than that, and then they would have taken thee for a friend. And had it not been that We had already made thee firm, thou wouldst certainly have been near to incline to them a little.[46]

The Prophet's firm conviction in his final triumph at the time of the severest opposition, when there was not a ray of hope otherwise,

---

46. 17:73, 74

may be read through every page of the Holy Quran. To the Prophet the Quran was the great spiritual force bound to conquer the whole world: "And if there were a Quran with which the mountains could be made to pass away or the earth could be travelled over or the dead were made to speak; nay, the command is entirely Allāh's".[47]

> Had We sent down this Quran on a mountain, thou wouldst certainly have seen it falling down, splitting asunder, because of the fear of Allāh, and We set forth these parables to men thay they may reflect.[48]

All opposition to the great truth which he had been appointed to establish was to him a passing phase. Thus in the earliest revelations:

> And bear patiently what they say and avoid them with a becoming avoidance. And leave Me and those who reject the truth, the possessors of ease and plenty, and give them a little respite.[49]

> Pharaoh disobeyed the Messenger, so We laid on him a violent hold. How then will you guard yourselves, if you disbelieve, on the day which will make children grey-headed? The heaven shall rend asunder thereby; His promise is ever brought to fulfilment.[50]

> And for the sake of thy Lord, be patient. For when the trumpet is sounded, That at that time, shall be a difficult day, For the unbelievers, anything but easy; Leave Me (to deal with) him whom I created alone, Then gave him vast riches, And sons dwelling in his presence, And I adjusted affairs for him adjustably, And yet he is greedy that I should give him more! By no means! he offers opposition to Our communications. I will make a distressing punishment overtake him.[51]

The strong faith that all opposition to his mission would fail and that he would succeed in bringing about the reformation with which

---

47. 13:31   48. 59:21   49. 73:10, 11   50. 73:16-18
51. 74:7-17

he was charged runs through every line of the Holy Quran, and the stronger the opposition grew the deeper became his faith in his ultimate success and of the failure of opposition. In another early revelation, it is said, after speaking of Pharaoh and other opponents of the truth:

> We overtook them after the manner of a Mighty, Powerful One. Are your unbelievers better than these or is there an exemption for you in the Scriptures? Or do they say, We are a host allied together to help each other. Soon shall the hosts be routed and they shall turn their back. Nay, the hour is their promised time, and that hour shall be most grievous and bitter.[52]

The Prophet prayed the whole night at the battle of Badr when he saw his three hundred men, his total strength, in danger of being annihilated by one thousand strong and well-armed enemies, saying, "O Lord! I beseech Thee according to Thy covenant and Thy promise," "O Lord! If such is Thy Will, Thou mayst not be served after this," "O Living, O Subsisting One by Whom all subsist! I crave for Thy mercy," and so on; and ultimately he came out of his hut reciting the above Quranic verses, showing that, notwithstanding the disparity of numbers and the utter weakness of his men, he was full of faith that this Divine promise was going to be fulfilled on that field. In fact, it was his strong faith in God that bore him up not only during the severest persecutions and trials at Mecca, but also during actual conflicts with the enemy in the battlefields around Medina when in numbers the Muslims were no match for the huge invading forces.

That all attempts at the reformation of Arabia before his appearance had failed, he knew for certain, but he was also certain that he would succeed in reclaiming not only the idolaters but also the spoiled followers of the Book:

> Those who disbelieved from among the followers of the Book and the idolaters could not have obtained freedom

---

52. 54:42-46

from sin until there had come to them the clear proof, A
Messenger from Allāh, reciting pure pages, Wherein are all
the right Books.[53]

If their hearts were hard as stones, or even harder than stones, he
was yet hopeful that he would make streams flow from these stones
and they would ultimately bow before God: "Then your hearts
hardened after that, so they were like rocks, nay harder still, and
there are rocks from which rivers gush, and there are some of them
which split asunder and water flows from them, and there are some
of them which fall down from fear of Allāh."[54]

The Prophet was, however, not only confident that his message
would breathe life into Arabia; he had a still deeper faith that he had
a message for the whole of humanity and that it was bound to
succeed in the end. His idea of the Divine plan for the uplift of
humanity was not limited to any one nation or any one generation.
His well-known prayer, which is now the prayer of millions of his
followers, five times a day, begins with the words:

All praise is due to Allāh, the Nourisher to perfection of all
nations.[55]

This was, therefore, the basis of his religion. According to him
the Divine plan was gradually to bring the whole of humanity to
perfection. He was not raised as a Messenger for the Arabs only; he
was the Messenger of God for the whole of humanity:

Say, O people! I am the Messenger of Allāh to you all, of
Him Whose is the kingdom of the heavens and the earth.[56]

And We have not sent thee but as a mercy to the nations.[57]

Blessed is He Who sent down the Furqān upon His servant
that he might be a warner to the nations.[58]

---

53. 98:1-3   54. 2:74

55. The Arabic word used here is Rabb which, according to the best authorities on
     Arabic Lexicology, means *fostering of a thing in such a manner as to make it
     attain one condition after another until it reaches its goal of completion*, and
     includes both the physical and the spiritual phases of life.

56. 7:158   57. 21:107   58. 25:1

And in the earliest revelations: "And it is naught but a reminder to the nations."[59]

It shows a boundless faith in his ultimate triumph to reform the whole of humanity when it is repeated thrice: "He it is Who has sent His Messenger with the guidance and the religion of truth that He may cause it to prevail over all the religions."[60]

If a deep-rooted faith in God was the secret of the Prophet's own wonderful success, it was also the foundation-stone of the great reformation which he brought about. He did not start by applying himself to this or that vice or superstition or degrading usage or evil custom; he applied himself, first of all, solely to grounding men in faith in God. Almost the whole of his Mecca revelation has but one theme: God is the Creator of all, He is the Nourisher of all, He reveals Himself to man, He makes His will known to man, He is the Holy One, He is nearer to man than his own soul, He is the Beneficent One, the Merciful One, the Loving One, the Affectionate, the Forgiving One, the Giver of all gifts, the Ample-giving, He listens to every man's prayer, He loves good and hates evil, He loves those who serve the poor and those in distress, He loves the truthful ones, and so on.

The man who has faith in God is like a live wire and those who come in contact with him, imbibe faith from him. Full of faith as the Prophet's own heart was, full to overflowing, it had a magic effect on those who came in contact with him, and their hearts were filled with the same strong faith. The current of faith which was thus transmitted from the heart of the Prophet to the hearts of those who sat at his feet was further strengthened by the constant stress which revelation laid on the existence of God. The whole of nature testified to the existence of God:

> Do they not look up to the heaven above them, how We have made it and adorned it and it has no gaps. And the earth We have spread it forth and cast upon it mountains and We have made to grow therein of all beautiful kinds, To give

---

59. 68:52; 81:27 60. 9:33; 48:28; 61:9

sight and as a reminder to every servant who turns (to God) again and again! And from the cloud We send down water abounding in good, then We cause to grow thereby gardens and grain that is reaped, and the tall palm-trees having spadices closely set one above another, A sustenance for the servants, and We give life thereby to a dead land; thus is the resurrection.[61]

What is the matter with you that you hope not for greatness from Allāh? And indeed He has created you through various grades.[62] Do you not see how Allāh has created the seven heavens alike, And made the moon therein a light and made the sun a lamp? And Allāh has made you grow out of the earth as a growth, Then He returns you to it, then will He bring you forth a (new) bringing forth. And Allāh has made for you the earth a wide expanse, That you may go along therein in wide paths.[63]

Who created death and life that He may try you - which of you is best in deeds; and He is the Mighty, the Forgiving; Who created the seven heavens alike; thou seest not incongruity in the creation of the Beneficent God; then look again, canst thou see any disorder? Then turn back the eye again and again, thy look shall come back to thee confused while it is fatigued.[64]

In the creation of the heavens and the earth, and the alternation of the night and the day, and the ships that run in the sea with that which profits men, and the water that Allāh sends down from the clouds, then gives life with it to the earth after its death, and spreads in it all kinds of animals,

---

61. 50:6-11
62. These words imply that man has been brought to the present state of physical perfection after passing through various conditions and contain an allusion to the theory of evolution.
63. 71:13-20
64. 67:2-4. The oneness of law in the whole universe is referred to as an argument for the unity of God.

and the changing of the winds and the clouds made subservient between the heaven and the earth, these are signs for a people who understand.[65]

Such were the arguments drawn from the material universe that it must have a Creator. Another class of arguments regarding the existence of God related to the human soul in which was implanted the consciousness of Divine existence. An appeal is again and again made to man's inner self:

Or were they created from nothing? Or are they the creators? Or did they create the heavens and the earth?[66]

Am I not your Lord?[67]

God-consciousness was thus shown to be part and parcel of human nature. Sometimes this consciousness is mentioned in terms of the unimaginable nearness of the Divine Spirit to the human spirit:

We are nearer to man than his life-vein.[68]

We are nearer to your soul than yourselves.[69]

This meant that the consciousness of the existence of God in the human soul was even clearer than the consciousness of its own existence. But it differed in different natures according as the inner light of man was bright or dim. Thus God was to the Muslim the central fact of human life, and he therefore turned to Him again and again to seek help and guidance from Him. Faith in God assumed a practical shape in the form of prayer. Five times a day did he pray to God, the essential part of the prayer being the short Opening chapter of the Holy Quran:

All praise is due to Allāh, the Nourisher to perfection of the worlds,
Master of the day of requital.
Thee do we serve and Thee do we beseech for help.
Guide us on the right path,
The path of those upon whom Thou hast bestowed favours,

---

65. 2:164   66. 52:35, 36   67. 7:172   68. 50:16
69. 56:85

> Not of those upon whom wrath is brought down, nor of those who go astray.[70]

The yearning of man's soul after God is manifested in his prayer to God, but this yearning becomes more manifest when man finds himself in distress:

> And when distress afflicts a man, he calls upon his Lord, turning to Him frequently, and when He grants him a favour from Himself, he forgets that for which he called upon Him before.[71]

> When harm afflicts a man, he calls upon Us, and when We give him a favour from Us, he says, I have been given it only by means of (my) knowledge.[72]

> And when affliction touches a man, he calls on Us whether lying on his side or sitting or standing, but when We remove his affliction from him, he passes on as though he had never called on Us.[73]

Man was not only told to pray to God in all circumstances, in ease as well as in distress, and to seek help and guidance from Him on all occasions, but it was further impressed on him that God did listen to the prayer of man:

> And your Lord says: Call upon Me and I will answer you.[74]

> Who answers the distressed one when he calls upon Him and removes the evil, and He makes you rulers in the earth?[75]

> Surely My Lord is the Hearer of prayers.[76]

> And when My servants ask thee concerning Me, then surely I am very near; I answer the prayer of the suppliant when he calls on Me; so they should respond to Me and believe in Me that they may walk in the right way.[77]

He was further taught to rely on God in all circumstances so that he should not lose heart in failures and difficulty:

---

70. 1:1-7   71. 39:8   72. 39:49   73. 10:12
74. 40:60   75. 27:62   76. 14:39   77. 2:186

With none but Allāh is the direction of my affair to a right issue; on Him do I rely and to Him do I turn.[78]

And what reason have we that we should not rely on Allāh, and He indeed guides us in our ways, and certainly we would bear with patience your persecution of us, and on Allāh should the reliant rely.[79]

Rely on the Living One Who dies not and celebrate His praise, and Sufficient is He as being Aware of the faults of His servants.[80]

And whoever trusts in Allāh, He is Sufficient for him; surely Allāh attains His purpose. Allāh indeed has appointed a measure for everything.[81]

He was also taught to seek refuge in God whenever he found himself in danger of being led astray or in affliction:

I seek refuge in the Lord of men, the King of men, the God of men.[82]

O my Lord! I seek refuge in Thee from the evil suggestions of the evil ones, And I seek refuge in Thee, O my Lord! that they should be present with me.[83]

And if a false imputation from the evil one afflict thee, seek refuge in Allāh; surely He is Hearing, Knowing.[84]

In God was contentment of mind to be sought:

Those who believe and whose hearts are set at rest by the remembrance of Allāh; now surely in the remembrance of Allāh do hearts find rest.[85]

God was indeed the Creator and the Ruler Supreme, but He was also the Friend of Man:

And surely the unjust are friends of each other, and Allāh is the Friend of those who have regard for their duty.[86]

---

78. 11:88; 13:30   79. 14:12   80. 25:58   81. 65:3
82. 114:1-3   83. 23:97, 98   84. 7:200   85. 13:28
86. 45:19

Or have they taken guardians besides Him? But Allāh is the Guardian-Friend, and He gives life to the dead and He has power over all things.[87]

Allāh is the Friend of those who believe; He brings them out of darkness into the light.[88]

And Allāh is sufficient as a Friend, and Allāh is sufficient as a Helper.[89]

The kindness and mercy of God are boundless, beyond the conception of man; He is Merciful to the believers and to the unbelievers, to the righteous and to the sinners alike:

O My servants who have acted extravagantly against their own souls! Do not despair of the mercy of Allāh, for Allāh forgives the sins altogether.[90]

Our Lord! Thou embracest all things in mercy and knowledge.[91]

Say, in the grace of Allāh and His mercy, in that they should rejoice.[92]

Except those on whom Thy Lord has mercy, and for this did He create them.[93]

Despair not of Allāh's mercy, for none despairs of Allāh's mercy except the unbeliever.[94]

He has ordained mercy on Himself.[95]

Your Lord is the Lord of all-encompassing mercy.[96]

And My mercy encompasses all things.[97]

And if you count Allāh's favours, you will not be able to number them.[98]

---

87. 42:9   88. 2:257   89. 4:45   90. 39:53
91. 40:7   92. 10:58   93. 11:119   94. 12:87
95. 6:12, 54   96. 6:147   97. 7:156   98. 14:34; 16:18

Surely thy Lord is full of goodness towards men, though most of them are ungrateful.[99]

The very first revelation that came to the Prophet, and that commissioned him with the task of the reformation of mankind, speaks of the love of God which brought about the creation of Man:

Recite in the name of the Lord Who created.

He created man out of love,

Recite and thy Lord is the most Bounteous.[100]

In a saying of the Prophet, God is spoken of as saying:

I desired that I should be known, so I created man.

Wadūd, or the Loving God, is one of the attributes of the Divine Being:

He it is Who originates and reproduces, And He is the Forgiving, the Loving.[101]

Surely my Lord is Merciful, Loving.[102]

It is the attribute of love in the Divine nature that is reflected in man's love to God:

And they give away food out of love for Him to the poor and the orphan and the captive.[103]

And there are some men who set up equals with Allāh - they love them as they ought to love Allāh - and those who believe are stronger in their love for Allāh.[104]

Say, if you love Allāh, then follow me, Allāh will love you.[105]

God being Holy and Good, there is a special manifestation of Divine love towards those who eschew evil and do good:

Allāh loves those who do good to others.[106]

---

99. 27:73   100. 96:1-3   101. 85:13, 14   102. 11:90
103. 76:8   104. 2:165   105. 3:31
106. 2:195; 3:134, 148

Allāh loves those who turn much to Him and He loves those who purify themselves.[107]

Allāh loves the patient ones.[108]

Allāh loves those who fulfil their duty.[109]

Allāh loves those who judge equitably.[110]

Interwoven with the basic principle of faith in God is the great idea of the accountability of human actions. Every good deed has its reward, and every evil deed has its requital. Every man is responsible to God for what he does. In fact, man's highest responsibility is not to society or to the State but to God:

Every soul is held in pledge for what it earns.[111]

He Who has done an atom's weight of good shall see it, and he who has done an atom's weight of evil shall see it.[112]

And We have made every man's actions to cling to his neck, and We will bring forth to him on the Resurrection day a book which he will find wide open. Read thy book; thine own self is sufficient as a reckoner against thee this day. Whoever goes aright, for the benefit of his own soul does he go aright; and whoever goes astray, to its detriment does he go astray, and no bearer of a burden shall bear the burden of another.[113]

Everything done or said by man is preserved and bears its fruit; nothing is wasted:

Nay! But you give the lie to the judgment. And surely there are guardians over you, Honourable recorders; They know what you do.[114]

When the two receivers receive, sitting on the right and on the left. He utters not a word but there is by him a watcher at hand.[115]

---

107. 2:222   108. 3:146   109. 3:76; 9:4, 7   110. 5:42
111. 74:38   112. 99:7, 8   113. 17:13-15   114. 82:9-12
115. 50:17, 18

Or do they think that We do not hear what they conceal and their secret discourses? Aye! and Our messengers with them write down.[116]

This is Our book that speaks against you with justice; surely We wrote what you did.[117]

And they will say, Ah! Woe to us! What a book is this! It does not omit a small thing nor a great, but numbers them all.[118]

A man is judged by the preponderance of good or evil in him, and it is in this connection that the setting up of a balance is spoken of:

And We will set up a just balance on the day of Resurrection, so no soul shall be dealt with unjustly in the least, and though there be the weight of a grain of mustard seed, We will bring it and Sufficient are We to take account.[119]

The measuring out on that day will be just; then as for those whose measure of good deeds is heavy, they shall be successful. And as for those whose measure of good deeds is light, these it is that have made their souls suffer loss.[120]

An action leaves its effect upon the doer as soon as it is done, for God is "Quick in reckoning."[121] That effect is not seen by the human eye, but will be palpably manifest on the day of Resurrection when man's vision becomes keener by the removal of his earthly environments:

Certainly thou wert heedless of it, but now We have removed from thee thy covering, so thy sight this day is sharp.[122]

On the day when hidden things shall be made manifest.[123]

---

116. 43:80   117. 45:29   118. 18:49   119. 21:47
120. 7:8, 9   121. 2:202; 3:19, 199   122. 50:22
123. 86:9

Thus God not only made man, but He also takes account of everything done by him, and this is really the essence of faith in God. It was this significance of faith in God which the Holy Quran stressed, and which the Prophet impressed upon his followers to bring about a transformation in their lives. While this was the basis of a future life, paradise and hell being only the ultimate manifestations of this great law of good and evil, life on this earth was also an expression of the same law, good leading to a good and evil leading to an evil end:

> Your striving is surely directed to various ends. So as for him who gives gifts and guards against evil, and accepts what is good, We will ease his way to the state of ease. And as for him who is niggardly and considers himself free from need (of God), and rejects what is good, We will ease his way to a difficult end; And his wealth will not avail him when he perishes.[124]

The law of good and evil applied not only to individuals but also to nations. Every nation had a book of deeds according to which it was judged in this very life:

> And thou shalt see every nation kneeling down; every nation shall be called to its book; this day you shall be requited for what you did. This is Our book that pronounces against you with truth; surely We were writing what you did.[125]

Faith in God, built up on these foundations, received further strength from the spiritual experience of humanity which was the surest evidence of the existence of God. God had been revealing himself in all ages to all nations; such was the broad basis of the Prophet's faith in God. Man could make all discoveries in the sphere of the finite and he could conquer all forces of nature, but God was Infinite; and outside the sphere of man's discoveries:

> Vision comprehends Him not, and He comprehends all vision.[126]

---

124. 92:4-11   125. 45:28, 29   126. 6:103

So out of His great mercy, He revealed Himself to man; He revealed Himself to man through His chosen servants in every age and in every country:

> Surely We have revealed to thee as We revealed to Noah and the prophets after him, and We revealed to Abraham and Ishmael and Isaac and Jacob and the tribes, and Jesus and Job and Jonah and Aaron and Solomon, and We gave to David a scripture. And We sent messengers We have mentioned to thee before and messengers We have not mentioned to thee.[127]

> And every nation had a messenger.[128]

> And there is not a people but a warner has gone among them.[129]

Only mortals to whom God revealed Himself were sent as reformers because none but a mortal could serve as a model for men:

> Had there been in the earth angels walking about as settlers, We would have sent to them from heaven an angel as a messenger.[130]

> And We did not send before thee any but men to whom We revealed. So ask the followers of the reminder if you do not know. And We did not give them bodies not eating food, and they were not to abide for ever.[131]

God had thus been revealing Himself to all nations, and Divine revelation was recognized as a universal fact. While revelation in its highest form - revelation through the Holy Spirit - was peculiar to prophets, in its lower forms - in the form of the infusion of an idea into the mind, of a dream, a vision or inspiration - revelation was granted to others as well, to men as well as to women:

> And it is not for any mortal that Allāh should speak to him except by infusing an idea into the mind or from behind a

---

127. 4:163, 164   128. 10:47   129. 35:24   130. 17:95
131. 21:7, 8

veil or by sending a messenger and revealing by His permission what He pleases. Surely He is Exalted, Wise.

And thus did We send to thee the Spirit by Our command; thou didst not know what the book was, nor what Faith was, but We made it a light, guiding thereby whom We please of Our servants, and thou truly showest the way to the right path.[132]

And We sent a revelation to Moses' mother, saying: Give him suck, and when thou fearest for him cast him into the river and do not fear nor grieve, for We will bring him back to thee and make him one of the messengers.[133]

And when I sent a revelation to the disciples (of Jesus), saying, Believe in Me and My messenger.[134]

Unbelieving people are also spoken of as seeing significant and truthful dreams - the lowest form of revelation. Thus in the history of Joseph:

And two youths entered the prison with him. One of them said, I saw myself pressing wine; and the other said, I saw myself carrying bread on my head of which birds ate.[135]

And the King said, I see seven fat kine which seven lean ones devoured, and seven green ears and (seven) other dry; O chiefs! Explain to me my dream.[136]

Both the youths and the King were unbelievers, and the three dreams were interpreted by Joseph as speaking of the future, being thus prophetical in their essence.

Revelation was thus a universal human experience, and in its lower forms, others than prophets had experience of it. There was one further fact in this connection on which the Prophet laid the greatest stress. Truth thus revealed to man through Divine messengers had Divine sanction behind it. Wherever and whenever a prophet appeared in the world, he stood in the minority of one to a

---

132. 42:51, 52   133. 28:7   134. 5:111   135. 12:36
136. 12:43

whole nation which not only rejected the truth revealed to him but
did its utmost to destroy him. But opposition to truth, however strong
it was, had always been brough to naught. Powerful rulers and
powerful nations were destroyed when they opposed the truth, and
the lonely messenger of God, persecuted by all, was made
triumphant and succeeded in establishing the truth:

> Hast thou not considered how thy Lord dealt with 'Ād, The
> people of Aram, possessors of lofty buildings, The like of
> which were not created in the lands; And with Thamūd, who
> hewed out the rocks in the valley; And with Pharaoh, the
> lord of hosts, Who committed inordinacy in the cities, So
> they made great mischief therein; Therefore thy Lord let
> down upon them a portion of the chastisement.[137]

> And those who disbelieved said to their messengers, We will
> drive you out of our land, or else you shall come back into
> our religion. So their Lord revealed to them: Certainly We
> will destroy the wrongdoers, and We will settle you in the
> land after them.[138]

> And truly We wrote in the Book after the reminder that the
> land - My righteous servants shall inherit it. In this is a
> message to a people who serve Us.[139]

> Then We said, Go ye both to the people who reject Our
> communications, so We destroyed them with utter
> destruction. And as to the people of Noah when they rejected
> the messengers, We drowned them and made them a sign for
> men, and We have prepared a painful chastisement for the
> unjust. And 'Ād and Thamūd and the dwellers of Rass and
> many generations between them. And to every one We gave
> examples and every one did We destroy with utter
> destruction.[140]

---

137. 89:6-13   138. 14:13, 14   139. 21:105, 106   140. 25:36-39

Then we made Our promise good to them, so We delivered them and whom We pleased, and We destroyed the extravagant.[141]

And how many a town which was iniquitous did We demolish, and We raised up after it another people.[142]

Say: The truth has come and falsehood vanished; surely falsehood is a vanishing thing.[143]

Nay! We cast the truth against the falsehood, so that it breaks its head, and lo! it vanishes.[144]

This spiritual experience of humanity, an experience to which sacred history bore testimony in every age and every country, was the crowning argument which grounded faith deep in the hearts of the Prophet's followers. And now in the person of the Prophet himself they had a further living experience, seeing with their own eyes how truth was gaining ground day by day in the face of the severest opposition, and how it ultimately swept away every vestige of falsehood from the vast peninsula of Arabia.

They were further trained from the first to obey every order of God in the form of the call to prayer. Five times a day in the midst of their daily work, the call went forth that they must give up all work and resort to the mosque to bow their heads before God, standing side by side, the master and the servant, the high and the low, the rich and the poor. "God is the Greatest" was the refrain of this call, and implicit obedience to the orders of God became ingrained in them. Faith in God was thus translated into practice, and willing and thorough submission to His orders became the rule of life for a Muslim.

This prepared the Prophet's way to a thorough reformation of those who accepted him as their guide. Every order which came from on High was to be obeyed implicitly. The why and wherefore of it was not questioned. It was God's order and must be obeyed. Deep-rooted faith in God had given them a new outlook on life. The iron

---

141. 21:9   142. 21:11   143. 17:81   144. 21:18

chains of customs and usages now appeared to them as threads which it did not require any great effort to break. One after another all such usages were swept away as the details of the new law came from on High. The new spirit not only changed the individual; it transformed society, and thus the whole nation.

The evil of drink is perhaps the hardest to combat. The United States tried to uproot it by law and failed hopelessly. The Arabs were addicted to it as much as any nation of to-day. It was towards the end of the Prophet's life that the order came:

> O you who believe! Intoxicants and games of chance and sacrificing to stones set up and dividing by arrows are only an uncleanness, the devil's work; shun it therefore that you may be successful. The devil desires only to cause enmity and hatred to spring up in your midst by means of intoxicants and games of chance and to keep you off from the remembrance of Allāh and from prayer; will you then desist?[145]

As these verses were promulgated and a crier went forth proclaiming that wine was prohibited, every jar of wine in a Muslim house was emptied of wine and broken into pieces, so that wine flowed in the streets of Medina like water. And to this day, the Muslims, in whatever country they may be living, are as a nation free from this evil to a far greater extent than any other nation. it was not only that evil usages and customs and evil habits were swept away, but faith had infused into the Arabs and later on into other nations that accepted the message of Islām, a new life which made them the vanguards of civilization, the torch-bearers of physical, moral and spiritual advancement in the world.

---

145. 5:90, 91

Chapter 3
The Oneness of Humanity

The idea of the oneness of humanity is the Prophet's unique contribution to human civilization, and it came as a natural sequel to that foundation-stone of his teachings, the Unity of God. A perusal of world history shows the idea of the whole of humanity being a single nation as first dawning upon the Prophet's mind. It was a revelation from on High in the truest sense of the word. No country was more unsuited than Arabia, either to give birth to such an idea or to see its accomplishment. The whole country was rent into innumerable petty states, each clan forming a separate and independent political unit. Each tribe had its own chief who would lead it in battle against a hostile tribe. The tribes and clans which inhabited that desert land were as loose as the sands of the desert. They were in the grip of unending feuds. The smallest thing served as a match to set ablaze the flames of war which lasted for years and years. There was wholesale bloodshed and destruction. Exhaustion would lead to forced treaties, but old grudges which kept smouldering would flare up again, and once more the country would find itself in the flames of war. The whole people were on the verge of being consumed to ashes by these flames of warfare:

> You were on the verge of a fiery abyss.[146]

Here dawned the idea for the first time in human history, not that the Arabs were one nation, but that the whole of humanity was a single nation:

> And people are naught but a single nation but they disagree.[147]

---

146. 3:103   147. 10:19

And this your community is one community and I am your
Lord, therefore have regard for your duty to Me. But they
became divided among themselves into parties, each party
rejoicing in that which is with them. So leave them in their
overwhelming ignorance till a time.[148]

This your community is one community only and I am your
Lord, therefore serve Me. And they cut off their affair
between them; to Us shall all come back.[149]

All people are a single nation; so Allāh raised prophets
(among all) bearing good news and giving warning, and He
revealed the Book with truth.[150]

It was not the momentary idea of a visionary thrown out in a
passing ecstasy; it was a principle of action worked out in all its
details in the revelations and practice of the Prophet. The division of
humanity into tribes and families was recognized, but the object of
this division was also the ultimate unification of humanity:

O you men! We have created you of a male and a female and
made you tribes and families that you may know each
other.[151]

The differences of colour and language were due to diversity in
nature:

And one of His signs is that He created you from dust, then
lo! you are mortals who scatter.[152]

And one of His signs is the creation of the heavens and the
earth, and the diversity of your tongues and colours; surely
there are signs in this for the learned.[153]

Whatever the country in which a people lived, whatever the
language they spoke, whatever the colour of their skins, they were all
recognized as one family living under one roof — the canopy of
heaven, and all enjoying equally the benefits of nature:

148. 23:52-54   149. 21:92, 93   150. 2:213   151. 49:13
152. 30:20   153. 30:22

O People! Fulfil your duty to your Lord Who created you
from a single being and created its mate of the same kind,
and spread from these two many men and women.[154]

And He it is Who made the stars for you that you might
follow the right way thereby in the darkness of the land and
the sea ... And He it is Who has brought you into being
from a single soul, then there is for you a resting-place and
a depository ... And He it is Who sends down water from
the clouds, then We bring forth with it the buds of all
plants.[155]

O men! Serve your Lord Who created you and those before
you so that you may guard against evil, Who made the earth
a resting-place for you and the heaven a canopy, and Who
sends down rain from the cloud then brings forth with it
subsistence for you of the fruits.[156]

The physical laws of God, it was thus taught, worked equally for
the whole of humanity and God was recognized as the Nourisher of
all; He was the Nourisher equally of the believers and of the
unbelievers:

Do you dispute with Us about Allāh, and He is our
Nourisher and your Nourisher, and we shall have our deeds
and you shall have your deeds.[157]

If the whole of humanity was one, because it enjoyed equally all
the benefits of nature, it was also one in receiving the spiritual
benefits of God. Prophets had been raised in every nation for their
spiritual welfare:

There is not a people but a warner has gone among
them.[158]

And every nation had a messenger.[159]

And every nation had a guide.[160]

---

154. 4:1   155. 6:98-100   156. 2:21, 22   157. 2:139
158. 35:24   159. 10:47   160. 13:7

> And certainly We raised in every nation a messenger, saying, Serve Allāh and shun the devil.[161]
>
> To every nation We appointed acts of devotion which they observe.[162]
>
> For every one of you did We appoint a law and a way.[163]

And finally there was but one law by which all people were to be judged; it was the law of deeds, every one being recompensed according to what he did:

> He who has done an atom's weight of good shall see it. And he who has done an atom's weight of evil shall see it.[164]
>
> Say, O unbelievers! ... You shall have your recompense and I shall have my recompense.[165]
>
> And if they call thee a liar, say: My work is for me and your work is for you; you are clear of what I do and I am clear of what you do.[166]
>
> I believe in what Allāh has revealed to me of the Book, and I am commanded to do justice between you; Allāh is our Lord and your Lord; We shall have our deeds and you shall have your deeds.[167]

A greater achievement of the Prophet than the laying down of the above noble precepts relating to the oneness of humanity is their translating into practice. This was a very tough job. The Arabs had as strong race and colour prejudices as any modern white nation, and a far stronger language prejudice. To all non-Arabs they gave the name 'Ajam, which meant *a mute people*, or *a people who could not express themselves well*, and 'ajmā meant *speechless animal* or *brute*. Thus all non-Arabs were looked down upon as more or less mute like animals, and unable to express their ideas in good language. Notwithstanding the fact that Arabia was partly under the heel of the Romans and partly under the heel of the Persians, the

---

161. 16:36   162. 22:67   163. 5:48   164. 99:7, 8
165. 109:1, 6   166. 10:41   167. 42:15

Arabs regarded themselves as a much superior race. As regards the Negroes, they did not recognize them except as slaves. The immediate task before the Prophet was therefore to blot out the race, colour and language prejudices from the Arab mind, as the Arab was to be the torch-bearer of the light to the rest of the world. The Muslims met together five times daily in prayer, and it was here that the levelling influence of Islām was first brought to bear. Among the first Muslims were the members of the noblest Quraish families as well as a goodly number of Negro slaves, and in the place of prayer and in the Prophet's company no difference of status was recognized between the two. From standing side by side in the ranks of prayer, the next step was a mere corollary: they mingled freely on terms of perfect equality on all other occasions. Service to God was thus the door through which the fraternization of humanity was effected. The Quraish would not sit in the Prophet's company because, they said, he mixed freely with what they considered lower strata of society. It was the Prophet's story that was being related in the story of Noah:

> We do not see any have followed thee but those who are the meanest of us at first thought.[168]

> I am not going to drive away those who believe; surely they shall meet their Lord; but I see that you are an ignorant people.[169]

> Nor do I say about those whom your eyes hold in mean estimation that Allāh will not grant them any good — Allāh knows best what is in their minds — for then surely I should be of the unjust.[170]

The Prophet himself is thus addressed:

> And withhold thyself with those who call on their Lord morning and evening, desiring His good will, and let not thine eyes pass from them, desiring the beauties of this world's life; and do not follow the desire of him whose heart We have made unmindful of Our remembrance.[171]

---

168. 11:27   169. 11:29   170. 11:31   171. 18:28

Thus the Negro slaves and the noble Quraish were made to meet together on terms of equality in prayer and in religious gatherings. They were all equal before God, it was thus impressed on their minds, and this they could easily understand. Life once moulded on these lines led to the natural consequence that the Negro slaves and the noble Quraish enjoyed equal status in society, and therefore both respected each other. The principle was further laid down that no one was to be honoured because he belonged to a particular race or a particular family or spoke a particular language or had a particular colour; honour was due to him who had the greatest regard for his duty:

> O you men! We have created you of a male and a female, and made you tribes and families that you may know each other; the most honourable of you with Allāh is the one among you who has the greatest regard for his duty.[172]

The *Imām* or the spiritual head of a congregation was to be chosen not because he belonged to a particular family but because he had a greater knowledge of the Holy Quran. The Prophet said:

> The man who knows most the Book of Allāh shall act as Imām of the people.[173]

> The most virtuous among you shall deliver the adhān and those having most knowledge of the Quran shall act as imāms.[174]

A Negro slave, Bilāl, was chosen by the Prophet himself to deliver the adhān in his own mosque, he himself being the Imām. Thus of the two office-bearers of the mosque, the Prophet himself was one, the other being Bilāl, a Negro.

Inter-dining and inter-marriages between Arabs and non-Arabs, even Negroes, were commonly resorted to, and the crowning act leading to the oneness of humanity in practice was that even a Negro could be placed in authority over the Arab. The Prophet said:

---

172. 49:13   173. Mishkāt, 4:26   174. Mishkāt, 4:26

Hear and obey, though a Negro whose head is like a raisin is entrusted with authority.[175]

---

175. Bukhārī, 10:54

CHAPTER 4
The Dignity of Manhood

Another unique contribution made by the prophet to human civilization was the idea of human dignity. This, too, was a natural sequel to the idea of the oneness of God, on which he laid so much stress. Man was the noblest of God's creation, according to the Prophet, and it was degrading for him to worship things or to bow before things which he really excelled:

> What! Shall I seek for you an object of worship other than Allāh, while He has made you excel all created things?[176]

That was to be the essential principle in man's relations with the rest of creation; he had been made to excel all things. He excelled even the angels, as the angels are required to make obeisance to man:

> And when We said to the angels, Make obeisance to Adam, they did obeisance.[177]

Man, therefore, degraded himself to the utmost if he carved out idols with his own hands and then worshipped them as if they were Divine, or as if they controlled good or evil for him:

> What! Do you serve what you hew out? And Allāh has created you and what you make.[178]

> Why dost thou worship that which neither hears, nor sees, nor does it avail thee in the least.[179]

The Prophet would not brook idolatry in any form. The association of anything with God made a man fall from the high position which nature had given him:

> Therefore avoid the uncleanness of idols and avoid false utterance — Being upright for Allāh, not associating aught

---

176. 7:140   177. 2:34   178. 37:95, 96   179. 19:42

69

with Him; and whoever associates others with Allāh, it is as though he had fallen from on high, then the birds snatch him away or the wind carries him off to a far distant place.[180]

He did not even allow great men to be taken as lords:

They have taken their doctors of law and their monks for lords besides Allāh, and also the Messiah, son of Mary, and they were commanded that they should serve one God only; there is no God but He.[181]

It was also a degradation of human nature that man should worship the sun or the moon or the stars or the elements of nature, because all these things were created for the service of man, and he was required to yoke them into service and control them:

Allāh is He Who made subservient to you the sea that the ships may run therein by His command and that you may seek of His grace.[182]

And the changing of the winds and the clouds made subservient between the heaven and the earth.[183]

He has made subservient to you the sun and the moon; each pursues its course till an appointed time.[184]

And He has made subservient to you the night and the day and the sun and the moon, and the stars are made subservient by His command.[185]

And He has made subservient to you whatsoever is in the heavens and whatsoever is in the earth, all, from Himself.[186]

According to the Prophet, man's position in nature was that of a conqueror; he had been created to control all the forces of nature and to rule in the earth, not to bow before them:

And when Thy Lord said to the angels, I am going to place in the earth one who shall rule in it.[187]

---

180. 22:30, 31   181. 9:31   182. 45:12   183. 2:164
184. 31:29   185. 16:12   186. 45:13   187. 2:30

He had been given vast capabilities for attaining the knowledge of things:

> And He gave Adam knowledge of all things.[188]

The Arabs were an illiterate people; reading and writing was so rare among them that it may be said not to have existed at all:

> And say to those who have been given the Book and the illiterate people: Do you submit yourselves (to God)?[189]

> He it is who raised among the illiterates a Messenger from among themselves.[190]

The followers of the Book, the Jews and the Christians, also gave the same name to the Arabs:

> This is because they say: There is not upon us any reproach in the matter of the illiterate people.[191]

The Prophet himself did not know reading and writing and is called an Unlearned Prophet:

> And thou didst not recite before it any book, nor didst thou transcribe one with thy right hand.[192]

> Those who follow the Messenger-Prophet, the unlearned one, whom they find written with them in the Torah and the Gospel, who enjoins them good and forbids them evil, and makes lawful to them the good things and makes unlawful to them impure things, and removes from them their burden and the shackles which were upon them.[193]

> Believe in Allāh and His Messenger, the unlearned Prophet, who believes in Allāh and His words, and follow him so that you may walk in the right way.[194]

Yet what was the very first message of this Unlearned Prophet who appeared among an illiterate people:

> Read in the name of thy Lord Who creates.[195]

---

188. 2:31   189. 3:19   190. 62:2   191. 3:74
192. 29:48   193. 7:157   194. 7:158   195. 96:1

> Read and thy Lord is most Bounteous, Who taught by the pen taught man what he knew not.[196]

Read and write, was thus his first message, and to these two means for gaining knowledge of things was added the quality of observation with which man was endowed:

> And how many a sign in the heavens and the earth which they pass by, yet they turn aside from it.[197]

> In the creation of the heavens and the earth and the alternation of the night and the day, there are surely signs for men of understanding: Those who remember Allāh standing and sitting and lying on their sides, and reflect on the creation of the heavens and the earth: Our Lord! Thou has not created this in vain.[198]

The knowledge of things thus gained was perfectly reliable because one law prevailed thoughout the vast universe whose extent could not be imagined by man:

> Thou seest no incongruity in the creation of the Beneficent God; then look again, canst thou see any disorder? Then turn back the eye again and again, thy look shall come back to thee confused while it is fatigued.[199]

Everything created by God, we are further told, was made according to a measure so that it could not go beyond a certain limit, and the progress made by every thing was along a certain line by following which it attained the perfection destined for it:

> Glorify the name of thy Lord, the Most High, Who creates things, then makes them complete; And Who makes things according to a measure, then guides them to their goal.[200]

From the slave of nature's forces which man generally was at that stage of human civilization, the Prophet thus raised him to the dignity of the master and the ruler, and it was due to this realization of man's position in the universe that the Muslims in their very early

---

196. 96:3-5   197. 12:105   198. 3:190, 191   199. 67:3, 4
200. 87:1-3

history took vigorous strides towards the expansion of knowledge and the advancement of the sciences. Reading and writing was within a few years spread throughout the whole of Arabia and other countries which came under the influence of Islām, and the Muslim State so encouraged the pursuit of study and scientific research that centres of learning and universities sprang up throughout the empire of Islām.

Along with this contribution to human thought in the physical sphere, a change was brought about in the spiritual outlook of man. The first change effected in this direction was that in the natural state man was pure; and every child whether born of Muslim or non-Muslim parents was sinless:

> Surely we have created man in the best make.[201]

> So set thy face upright for religion in the right state — the nature made by Allāh in which He has made men; there is no altering of Allāh's creation; that is the right religion but most people do not know.[202]

Explaining this verse of the Holy Quran, the Prophet is reported to have said:

> Every child that is born conforms to the true religion (lit., human nature); it is his parents who make him a Jew or a Christian or a Magian.[203]

Every child was thus recognized by birth to be a Muslim; the purity of human nature was not affected by his being born of non-Muslim parents. Hence it was further recognized that all children who died before attaining the age of discretion, whether they were children of Muslims or polytheists, went to heaven. On a certain occasion, the Prophet related a vision in which he had seen Abraham in paradise with children all around him, and he added that these children were all the children that had died in the state of nature, i.e. before they attained the age of discretion. Some of his companions, the Ḥadīth goes on to say, thereupon asked him:

---

201. 95:4   202. 30:30   203. Bukhārī, 23:80

The children of those who set up gods with God (mu<u>sh</u>rikīn) as well, O messenger of Allāh?

And he replied:

Yes, the children of those who set up gods with God (mu<u>sh</u>rikīn) as well.[204]

The doctrine of the sinlessness of man by birth was an aid to leading a sinless life. If a man did good and avoided evil he was true to his nature, while if he went against good and did evil he was false to his nature. It further strengthened him to overcome sin, because he knew that nature had fitted him for this task. But there was yet a further step to raise him spiritually to a very high level.

According to the Prophet not only no impurity attached to man in the natural state, i.e. by birth, but he, in a certain sense, also partook of the Divine nature, for it was the Divine Spirit that was breathed into man, into every human child:

Who made good everything that He created, and He began the creation of man from dust; Then He made his progeny of an extract, of water held in light estimation; Then He made him complete and breathed into him of His spirit.[205]

When thy Lord said to the angels, I am going to create a mortal from dust; so when I have made him complete and breathed into him of My spirit, fall down making obeisance to him.[206]

Evidently, the Divine Spirit spoken of here is something distinct from the animal soul which animates the whole animal kingdom, including man. It shows a mystic relation of the spirit of man with the Divine Spirit, and refers to the higher life of man. This was also the reason that God revealed Himself to the perfect Man in His full resplendence, and Divine revelation thus granted to man awakened him to a higher life and made him overcome his animal passions and low desires. The destiny of man, according to the Prophet, was

---

therefore higher than mere conquest of nature; it was to seek union with the Divine Spirit:

> O soul that art at rest! Return to thy Lord, well-pleased with Him, well-pleasing Him, So enter among My servants, And enter into My Garden.[207]

The goal of life was *liqā-Allāh*, or the meeting of God, in the language of the Holy Quran:

> O man! Thou must strive to attain to thy Lord a hard striving until thou meet Him.[208]

> They are losers indeed who reject the meeting of Allāh.[209]

> They will perish indeed who call the meeting of Allāh to be a lie.[210]

> He regulates the affair, making clear the signs that you may be certain of meeting your Lord.[211]

> And surely most of the people are deniers of the meeting of their Lord.[212]

The sublime thought that this worldly life was not the end and aim, nor conquest of nature the great goal of life, but that there were higher values of life, and that the present life was but a means to realize those values, the goal being a re-union with the Divine Spirit, this formed the basis of a life after death. The two lives, life on this earth and life beyond, are really one:

> Whoever is blind in this life, shall also be blind in the Hereafter.[213]

> And He shall cause them to enter the garden which he has made known to them (here).[214]

It is God's pleasure that a man is told to seek in this life, and God's pleasure is the greatest of the blessings of the next life:

---

207. 89:27-30   208. 84:6   209. 6:31   210. 10:45
211. 13:2   212. 30:8   213. 17:72   214. 47:6

Allāh has promised to the believing men and the believing
women gardens in which rivers flow, to abide in them, and
goodly dwellings in gardens of perpetual abode; and greatest
of all is Allāh's goodly pleasure — that is the grand
achievement.[215]

And as the believers do here below, they shall there glorify and
praise God:

Their cry in it shall be, Glory to Thee, O Allāh! And their
greeting in it shall be, Peace; and the last of their cry shall
be, Praise be to Allāh, the Lord of the worlds.[216]

This last cry of the life hereafter is also the first cry of the
Muslim in this life when he prays to God, at various times:

All praise is due to Allāh, the Lord of the worlds.[217]

The realization of the spiritual, however, is limited here owing
to the earthly environment, while the next life opens out unlimited
fields of advancement to higher and higher stages:

But those who fulfil their duty to their Lord shall have high
places built for them, above them higher places still.[218]

O you who believe! Turn to Allāh a sincere turning; maybe
your Lord will remove from you your evil and cause you to
enter gardens in which rivers flow, on the day on which
Allāh will not abase the Prophet and those who believe with
him; their light shall run on before them and on their right
hands; they shall say, Our Lord! Make perfect for us our
light and grant us protection, for Thou hast power over all
things.[219]

Paradise was thus, according to the Prophet, the starting point for
an advancement to higher and higher spiritual stages; hence the high
places to which the faithful shall be raised know no end, as there are
still higher places above them, and hence the ardent desire for more
and more light in that life.

---

215. 9:72   216. 10:10   217. 1:1   218. 39:20
219. 66:8

Even those who wasted their opportunity in this life by engrossment in lower desires would ultimately be saved, hell being only a remedial stage in the higher life of man. It is called a *maula*, or *friend*, of the sinners in one place,[220] and their *umm*, or *mother*, in another.[221]

All men, both believers and unbelievers, were created for mercy,[222] and the purpose of God must ultimately be fulfilled. They shall have a hard life in hell because they avoided here the "hard striving" which was needed to enable them to "meet their Lord."[223] All men will ultimately be made fit for the service of the Lord, because He had "not created the jinn and the men except that they should serve Me."[224] And the Prophet is reported to have said:

> Surely a day will come over hell when there shall not be a single human being in it.[225]

> Surely a day will come over hell when it will be like a field of corn that has dried up after flourishing for a while.[226]

---

220. 57:15   221. 101:9   222. 11:119   223. 84:6

224. 51:56   225. Fath al-Boyān fī Maqāṣid al-Qur'ān

226. Kanz al-'Ummāl

CHAPTER 5
Prayer to God

Another unique service the Prophet rendered to humanity was that he made prayer to God not only the foundation-stone of the individual development of man, but also the basis of the vast brotherhood of humanity which he established through Islām. The first three commandments which, he said, he had received from on High, were in the following order. Read and write, to attain to a place of honour, was, as we have already seen, his very first revelation. His second revelation was a command to warn the people and declare the greatness of God:

> O thou enveloped in thy garment! Arise and warn, And thy Lord do magnify.[227]

The third commandment, his third revelation in the historical order, was to pray to God; not only to pray to Him in the daytime but even during the night:

> O thou who hast wrapped up thyself! Keep awake in the night for prayer except a little, Half of it or lessen it a little, Or add to it and recite the Quran, reciting it in slow measured accents.[228]

Further on in the same chapter, we are told, how the Prophet himself and his companions kept this commandment:

> Surely thy Lord knows that thou keepest awake praying nearly two thirds of the night, and (sometimes) a half of it, and (sometimes) a third of it, as also a party of those with thee.[229]

---

227. 74:1-3   228. 73:1-4   229. 73:20

And in another early *sūra*, it is stated that resort to prayer was ordered both in the daytime as well as during the night:

> Keep up prayer from the declining of the sun till the darkness of the night and the recital of the Quran at dawn; surely the recital of the Quran at dawn is witnessed. And during a part of the night, keep away sleep by means of prayer, beyond what is incumbent on thee; maybe thy Lord will raise thee to a position of great glory.[230]

Prayer to God in the daytime as also during the night was thus declared to be the means of the raising of man to a position of great glory. It was further stated that prayer had to be resorted to time after time:

> So glory be to Allāh when you enter upon the time of the evening and when you enter upon the time of the morning — And to Him belongs praise in the heavens and the earth — and in the afternoon and when you are at midday.[231]

Thus guided, the Prophet made prayer an institution to which he himself and his followers resorted at stated times. It was not left to the individual to find out a time now and then to pray to God when he felt himself free; prayer was interwoven with his daily work: a prayer in the morning when he rose from his bed; a prayer at lunch time, as an indication that if his body needed a diet, so did his spirit; a prayer in the afternoon when he retired from his daily work; a prayer at sunset and a prayer when going to bed, being the final act of the day's work.

The object aimed at was to deepen in the human heart the roots of God-consciousness, with which man was endowed by nature; to make him remember again and again that he owed a duty to his Maker; to call him back when he was in the midst of his worldly engagements and to usher him into the Divine Presence; to awaken in him in the midst of all the turmoils and agitations which were likely to lead his mind away from God, the consciousness that there

---

230. 17:78, 79   231. 30:17, 18

was a Higher Presence to Whom he was really responsible for what
he did; to remind him in the hour of triumph that he was nothing but
a weak and humble creature of God, and in the hour of his failure and
disappointment that he had still a support to fall back upon, and that
there was nothing to despair of.

The stress laid on prayer was due to the fact that it was, in the
first place, the means of realizing the Divine in man. The Prophet did
not deem it sufficient simply to preach the existence of God as a
theory. He sought to instil into man's mind the conviction that God
is, and to make it a living force in his life. The three requisites of a
Muslim are given in the beginning of the Holy Quran in their natural
order:

> This Book, there is no doubt in it, is a guide to those who
> fulfil their duty: Those who believe in the unseen and keep
> up prayer and spend out of what We have given them.[232]

Belief in God, the Great Unseen, is immediately followed by the
keeping up of prayer, thus showing that by means of prayer belief is
turned into a realization of the Divine within man, into a certainty of
the Divine existence; and this again is followed by spending out of
what God has given man, for the benefit of others in charity. Thus
faith in God is translated into practice by prayer, which, in its turn,
leads to the service of humanity. According to the Prophet, self-
development of man depended upon prayer:

> Successful indeed are the believers, Who are humble in their
> prayers.[233]

The Arabic word for success is *falāh* which means *the complete
attainment of what one desires*. To the Prophet *falāh* (or *success*) and
prayer were so closely connected that they might almost be regarded
as two interchangeable terms. Five times a day did he order the call
to go forth from the minaret of every mosque:

> Come to prayer   Come to prayer
> Come to success   Come to success.

---

232. 2:2, 3   233. 23:1, 2

It was again through prayer to God that man's heart was purified and the evil tendencies in him were suppressed:

> Recite that which has been revealed to thee of the Book and keep up prayer; surely prayer keeps one away from indecency and evil.[234]

> And keep up prayer in the two parts of the day and in the first hours of the night; surely good deeds take away evil tendencies.[235]

The Prophet explained further what the Holy Quran taught. On one occasion he thus addressed his companions:

> Tell me if there is a stream at the door of one of you in which he bathes five times daily; what dost thou say, will it leave anything of his dirt?

And on receiving the reply that it would not, he added:

> This is the likeness of the five prayers with which Allāh washes away all faults.[236]

With the Prophet prayer was an aspiration of the human spirit to be in touch with the Divine Spirit, the fountain-head of purity and the possessor of perfect attributes:

> All the perfect attributes are Allāh's.[237]

> His are the most excellent attributes.[238]

> Be imbued with the Divine morals.

The only way to do this was to get in touch with the Divine Spirit, to be drawn away from the imperfection of human environment for a while and to drink deep at the Divine fountain-head of purity and perfection. "When one of you," said the Prophet, "says his prayers, he holds confidential intercourse with his Lord."[239] In prayer, the Divine Presence was reality:

---

234. 29:45   235. 11:114   236. Bukhārī, 9:6   237. 7:180

238. 59:24   239. Bukhārī, 9:8

> Thou shouldst worship Allāh as if thou didst see Him; if thou dost not see Him, He surely sees thee.[240]

> And seek (Divine) help through patience and prayer, and surely it is a hard thing except for the humble ones, Who know that they shall meet their Lord, and that they shall return to Him.[241]

These descriptions of prayer show its real nature to be that of being in actual intercourse with the Divine Being, and the man who prays to Him in real earnest, prays to Him with the conviction that he can meet Him in this very life.

Prayer was further meant to seek help as well as guidance from God. The seeking of help and guidance is linked up in the daily prayer of the Muslim, repeated about forty times a day:

> Thee do we serve and of Thee do we seek help.
> Guide us on the right path.[242]

Thus, every now and then, the Muslim is required to turn to God to seek both help and guidance from Him in all his undertakings.

In one place, prayer is referred to as a sustenance for the spirit of man, so that the man who does not pray to God must be regarded as spiritually dead:

> And glorify thy Lord by the praising of Him before the rising of the sun and before its setting, and during the hours of night do also glorify Him and during parts of the day, that thou mayest be well-pleased. And do not stretch thy eyes after that with which We have provided different classes of men, and the sustenance of thy Lord is better and more abiding. And enjoin prayer on those dependent on thee and steadily adhere to it thyself; We do not ask thee for sustenance: We do give thee sustenance; and the good end is for those who fulfil their duty.[243]

---

240. Bukhārī, 2:37   241. 2:45, 46   242. 1:4, 5   243. 20:130-132

"That with which We have provided different classes of men," are things pertaining to the physical life of man, things which he needs physically, and in comparison with these prayer is called the "better and more abiding" "sustenance of thy Lord," a thing which man needs spiritually. Prayer is thus needed time after time, both during the day and the night, to sustain the spirit of man, as food is needed time after time to sustain the body.

The prayer service was divided by the Prophet into two parts, one to be said in private, and the other to be performed in congregation, preferably in a mosque. While the private part was meant simply for the development of the inner self of man, the public part had other ends as well in view — ends, indeed, that make the Islāmic prayer a mighty force in the unification of the human race. In the first place, this gathering of all people living in the same vicinity five times daily, is a help towards the establishment of healthy social relations. In the daily services these relations are limited to a comparatively narrow circle, i.e. to members of the same neighbourhood. The circle, however, becomes wider in the weekly Friday service which gathers together all Muslim members of a particular locality, and still more extensive in the two annual gatherings of the Muslim festival, called 'Id. Thus prayer promotes social relations between the different sections of the Muslim community.

Far more important than this, however, is the levelling of social differences brought about by means of congregational prayer. Once within the doors of the mosque, every Muslim feels himself in an atmosphere of equality and love. Before their Maker all Muslims were made to stand shoulder to shoulder, the king along with his humblest subject, the rich arrayed in costly robes with the beggar clad in rags, the white man along with the black one. There could be no greater levelling influence in the world. All men, great and small, white and black, stood on terms of perfect equality five times a day in the mosque and this entirely changed the mentality which made one man think himself superior to another, either on account of riches, or on account of rank, or on account of race or colour.

The congregational prayer, instituted by the Prophet, in fact, carried into practice the theoretical lessons of equality and fraternity, of the oneness of humanity, which he taught. However forcibly he may have preached in words the equality of man and the fraternity of the community of Islām, all this would have ended in mere talk had it not been translated into everyday life through the institution of the daily congregational prayers. Thus the institution of prayer as established by the Prophet became a unique force in the unification of the human race.

Congregational prayer effected yet another great purpose. Differences of rank, wealth, race and colour vanished within the mosque; and quite a new atmosphere, an atmosphere of brotherhood, equality and love prevailed within the holy precincts. It is indeed a blessing to be able to breathe, five times daily, in the atmosphere of perfect peace in a world of strife and struggle; of equality where inequality is the order of the day; and of love amid the petty jealousies and enmities of daily life. It is more than a blessing, for it is the great lesson of life. Man has to work amidst inequalities, amidst strife and struggle, amidst scenes of hatred and enmity; and yet he is drawn out of these five times a day and made to realize that equality, fraternity and love are the real sources of human happiness. The time spent in prayer is not, therefore, wasted even from the point of view of active humanitarianism; on the contrary, the best use of it is made in learning those great lessons which make life worth living. And these lessons of fraternity, equality and love, when put into practice in daily life, serve as foundations for the unification of the human race and for lasting civilization of mankind.

The Prophet went yet a step further. He taught that the prayerful attitude of man was not to be limited to the four walls of the mosque, nor to the particular condition when he was actually engaged in prayer. His programme was to make humanity prayer-minded, and so he taught a prayer with every change in man's mood. Though a Muslim's last act before going to bed is an organized prayer, yet when actually going to bed, he was taught a prayer which should set at rest all the anxieties of the day and the troubles of life, and help him in enjoying sound sleep with the assurance that he was a faithful servant of God:

> O Allāh! Into Thy charge do I give my soul, and into Thy hand do I entrust my affair, and to Thee do I turn my whole attention, and in Thee do I seek support for my back, longing for and fearing Thee; there is no refuge and no deliverance but in Thee; I believe in Thy book which Thou hast revealed and in Thy Prophet whom Thou hast sent.[244]

There was a different prayer on arising from sleep, so that while giving praise to God for another day of life, man should start the day with the conviction that his greatest responsibility was to God alone:

> All praise is due to Allāh Who raised us to life after He had caused us to die, and to Him is the rising. There is no God but Allāh; He is One, there is no associate with Him; His is the Kingdom and for Him is the praise, and He is powerful over all things.[245]

When a man went forth from his house for his business, he was taught to pray that in his dealings with others he might be just to them and that the All-Powerful God might withhold the hands of those who do injustice to Him:

> In the name of Allāh, on Allāh do I rely. O Allāh! We seek Thy refuge lest we stumble or go astray, or lest we do injustice to others or injustice is done to us, or lest we behave ignorantly towards others or others behave ignorantly towards us.[246]

And when he returned to his house after his day's business, with all his failures he should still rely on God and pray thus:

> O Allāh! I beseech Thee that I may be made to enter a goodly entering and to go forth a goodly going forth; in the name of Allāh do we enter, and on Allāh our Lord do we rely.[247]

---

244. Muslim Prayer Book, p. 50   245. *Ibid.*, p. 51   246. *Ibid.*, p. 51
247. *Ibid.*, p. 51

The blessing of God was to be sought before taking one's meals:

In the name of Allāh and with blessings from Allāh.[248]

And praise was to be given to Him after the meal was finished:

All praise is due to Allāh Who gave us to eat and to drink and He has made us Muslims.[249]

On going out on a journey, the deepest desire of the heart should be that one should be faithful to one's duty and do only that which is pleasing to God, and that God may grant safety to one's self as well as to those one has left behind:

O Allāh! We ask of Thee during this our journey righteousness and faithfulness to duty, and the doing of deeds Thou art pleased with. O Allāh! Thou art the companion in the journey and the guardian of the family.[250]

When entering a town, one should pray for the good of the town and the good of its residents:

O Allāh! We ask of Thee the good of this town and the good of its residents, and we seek refuge in Thee from its mischief and the mischief of its residents and the mischief of what is in it. O Allāh! Make its residents love us and make us love the righteous among its residents.[251]

When visiting a sick man, one should pray to God that health may be restored to him:

Take away the sickness, O Lord of all people! and restore (Thy servant) to health. Thou art the Healer; there is no healing but that which Thou grantest. Grant recovery which leaves no ailment behind.[252]

On entering a boat, one should seek the help of God for a safe sailing:

---

248. Muslim Prayer Book, p. 52   249. Ibid., p. 52   250. Ibid., p. 54
251. Ibid., p. 53   252. Ibid., p. 53

In the name of Allāh be its sailing and its anchoring; surely my Lord is Forgiving, Merciful.[253]

When riding or driving, one should give praise to God Who made man master of these things:

> Glory be to Him Who made this subservient to us, and we were not able to do it, and surely to our Lord we must return.[254]

When one has performed an external act of purification, he should pray to God for the purification of his soul:

> O Allāh! Make me of those who turn to Thee and make me of those who purify themselves.[255]

When facing the enemy, one should seek the refuge of Allāh:

> O Allāh! We beseech Thy help in opposing them and seek refuge in Thee from their mischiefs.[256]

The prayer for victory over an enemy stands unparalleled. It is always preceded by a desire for conquest of self and for humbleness:

> Our Lord! Do not punish us if we forget or make a mistake; our Lord! do not lay on us a burden as Thou didst lay on those before us; our Lord! do not impose on us that which we have not the strength to bear, and pardon us and grant us protection and have mercy on us, Thou art our Protecting Friend, so help us against the unbelieving people.[257]

> Our Lord! Forgive us our faults and our excess in our affairs and make firm our feet and help us against the unbelieving people.[258]

253. Muslim Prayer Book, p. 55   254. *Ibid.*, p. 54   255. *Ibid.*, p. 56
256. *Ibid.*, p. 56   257. 2:286   258. 3:146

Chapter 6
The Service of Humanity

In the earliest preachings of the Prophet as much stress was laid on prayer to God as on service to humanity, perhaps more on the latter. In fact, prayer to Him was meaningless if it was not accompanied with service to humanity. It would be a mere show, severely condemnable. One of the short, earliest, chapters is devoted entirely to this:

> Hast thou considered him who gives the lie to religion? That is the one who treats the orphan with harshness, And does not urge the feeding of the needy. So woe to those who pray, Who are heedless of their prayers, Who make a show of their prayers, And refuse small acts of kindness (to their fellow-beings).[259]

Prayer, therefore, had no value if it did not lead to the service of humanity. Of the two, prayer to God and service of humanity, the latter was the more difficult task. It was an uphill road:

> And (have We not) pointed out to man the two conspicuous ways? But he would not attempt the uphill road. And what will make thee comprehend what the uphill road is? It is the setting free of a slave, Or the giving of food in a day of hunger, To an orphan near of kin, Or to the needy one lying in the dust.[260]

The orphan and the needy were not only to be helped; they were to be honoured:

> Nay! But you do not honour the orphan; Nor do you urge one another to feed the needy; And you eat up the heritage,

---

259. 107:1-7   260. 90:10-16

devouring it indiscriminately; And you love wealth with exceeding love.[261]

Wealth was not given to man for amassing; the needy had a right in the wealth of rich:

And in their properties is a portion due to him who begs and to him who is denied (the fortunes of life).[262]

In a very early revelation, the possessors of wealth who do not help the poor are threatened with destruction:

We will try them as We tried the owners of the garden when they swore that they would cut the produce in the morning; And were not willing to set aside a portion for the needy. Then there encompassed it a visitation from thy Lord while they were sleeping; So it became as black, barren land. And they called out to each other in the morning: Go early to your tilth if you would cut the produce. So they went, saying in low tones one to another, No needy one shall enter it to-day upon you. And in the morning they went, having the power to prevent (the needy). But when they saw it, they said: Surely we have gone astray; Nay! we are deprived of everything.[263]

From his early life the Prophet was a staunch supporter of the cause of the weak and the oppressed. When quite young, he became a member of the Ḥilfal-Fudzūl, an alliance formed to vindicate the rights of the weak and the oppressed against tyranny. Each member of this alliance was bound in honour to defend the helpless against all manner of oppression. The credit of taking the lead in the formation of this humanitarian organization belonged to the Prophet and his family, the Banū Hāshim.

When deputation after deputation of the Quraish went to Abū Ṭālib to persuade him to deliver the Prophet to them to be put to death, Abū Ṭālib sang his praise in the memorable words which have come down to us in one of his poems. What! said he, shall I make

---

261. 89:17-20   262. 51:19   263. 68:17-27

over to you one "who is the refuge of the orphans and protector of the widows." And when on receiving the Call, Muḥammad trembled for fear that he might not be able to achieve the grand task of the reformation of humanity, his wife consoled him in these words:

> Nay, I call Allāh to witness that Allāh will never bring thee to disgrace, for thou unitest the ties of relationship and bearest the burden of the weak and earnest for the destitute and honourest the guest and helpest people in real distress.[264]

Human sympathy was implanted in the Prophet's very nature, so that he had not only a deep concern for the physical ills of humanity, but a still deeper concern for its moral degradation and spiritual fall. The Holy Quran bears clear witness to this:

> Perhaps thou wilt kill thyself with grief because they do not believe.[265]

> Maybe thou wilt kill thyself with grief, sorrowing after them if they do not believe in this announcement.[266]

When he rose to kingship, one of his first reforms was the suppression of the iniquitous law which deprived orphans and women of their share in inheritance. The Arabs had a strong tradition that "only he could inherit property who smites with the spear." In a country where fighting was going on day and night, the value of such a tradition cannot be overestimated. Yet it was at the very time when the Prophet stood in need of defenders of the community and the faith, that the law was laid down which abolished all such discriminations against the weak and the helpless, and placed the woman and the child on a par with the soldier who fought for their protection:

> Men shall have a portion of what the parents and the near relatives leave, and women shall have a portion of what the parents and the near relatives leave, whether there is little or much of it: a stated portion.[267]

---

264. Bukhārī, 1:1   265. 26:3   266. 18:6   267. 4:7

And give to the orphans their property, and do not substitute worthless things for their good ones, and do not devour their property as an addition to your own property; this is surely a great crime.[268]

I may add a few out of a large number of the Prophet's sayings which impressed upon his hearers that the service of humanity was a great goal of life:

Whoever does the needful for his brother, Allāh does the needful for him; and whoever removes the distress of a Muslim, Allāh removes for him a distress out of the distresses of the day of Resurrection.[269]

Thou wilt see the faithful in their having mercy for one another and in their love for one another and in their kindness towards one another; like the body — when one member of it ails, the entire body ails.[270]

Your slaves are your brethren; Allāh has placed them under your control; so whoever has his brother under his control, he should feed him from what he eats and should give him clothes to wear from what he wears; and do not impose on them a task which should overpower them; and if you do impose on them such a task, then help them in the doing of it.[271]

One who manages the affairs of the widow and the needy is like one who exerts himself hard in the way of Allāh, or one who stands up for prayer in the night and fasts in the day.[272]

I and the man who brings up an orphan will be in paradise like this. And he pointed with his two fingers, the forefinger and the middle finger.[273]

Allāh has no mercy on him who is not merciful to men.

---

268. 4:2   269. Bukhārī, 46:3 270. *Ibid.*, 78:27   271. *Ibid.*, 2:22

272. *Ibid.*, 69:1   273. *Ibid.*, 78:24

He is not of us who does not show mercy to our little ones and respect to our great ones.[274]

He had a tender heart even for animals. It is related that he passed by a camel that had grown extremely lean; so he said:

Be careful of your duty to Allāh regarding these dumb animals; ride them while they are in a fit condition, and eat them while they are in a fit condition.[275]

A prostitute was forgiven: she passed by a dog panting with its tongue out, on the top of a well containing water, almost dying with thirst, so she took off her boot and tied it to her head-covering and drew forth water for it; she was forgiven on account of this.

His companions asked: Is there a reward for us in doing good to beasts? He replied: "In every animal having a liver fresh with life, there is a reward."[276]

---

274. Mishkāt, 24:15   275. Abū Dāwood, 15:43
276. Mishkāt, 6:6

Chapter 7
Charity

The Prophet's charity was proverbial. He was not known to have ever said "No" to anyone who asked of him anything. "He was the most charitable of men," was the description of him given by his companions to later generations, and as if these words did not sufficiently express the Prophet's charity, it was added:

> The Messenger of Allāh, may peace and blessings of Allāh be on him, was more charitable than the wind which is sent forth on everybody.[277]

So full of charity himself, charity was, next to obedience to God, the theme on which he laid the greatest stress. The sum and substance of his religion has been rightly given as "Obedience to God and charity to man." This unparalleled love of charity both in example and precept proceeded from his immeasurable love for God. And he therefore preached that love of God should be the basis of charity. It is said in one of the earliest revelations:

> And they feed out of love for Him the needy and the orphan and the captive: We only feed you for the sake of Allāh; we desire from you neither reward nor thanks.[278]

And in a later revelation:

> Righteousness is this that one should believe in Allāh and the last day and the angels and the Book and the prophets, and give wealth out of love for Him to the near of kin and the orphans and the needy and the wayfarer and the beggars and for the emancipation of the captives.[279]

---

277. Bukhārī, 1:1   278. 76:8, 9   279. 2:177

> And the parable of those who spend their property to seek
> the pleasure of Allāh and for the strengthening of their souls
> is as the parable of a garden on elevated ground, upon which
> heavy rain falls, so it brings forth its fruit twofold; but if
> heavy rain does not fall upon it, then light rain is
> sufficient.[280]

Charity proceeding from such a pure motive brought about
increase of wealth:

> So give to the near of kin his due, and to the needy and the
> wayfarer; this is best for those who desire Allāh's pleasure,
> and these it is who are successful. And whatever you lay out
> at usury, so that it may increase in other people's property,
> it shall not increase with Allāh; and whatever you give in
> charity desiring Allāh's pleasure — these it is that shall get
> manifold increase.[281]

The increase which charity brought in its train is likened to the
seed which grows seven hundredfold and even multiples of seven
hundred:

> The parable of those who spend their property in the way of
> Allāh is as the parable of a grain growing seven ears with a
> hundred grains in every ear; and Allāh multiplies for whom
> He pleases; and Allāh is Ample-giving, Knowing.[282]

The exercise of charity must be free from show and from all
sordid motives, such as any personal gain or even placing the object
of charity under an obligation:

> Those who spend their property in the way of Allāh, then do
> not follow up with reproach or injury what they have spent,
> they shall have their reward from their Lord, and they shall
> have no fear nor shall they grieve. Kind speech and
> forgiveness is better than charity followed by injury; and
> Allāh is Self-sufficient, Forbearing. O you who believe! Do
> not make your charity worthless by reproach and injury, like

---

280. 2:265   281. 30:38, 39   282. 2:261

him who spends his property to make a show of it and does
not believe in Allāh and the last day; so his parable is as the
parable of a smooth rock with earth upon it, then a heavy
rain falls upon it so it leaves it bare.[283]

Charity must be given out of good things, out of things which a
man loves for himself:

O you who believe! Give in charity of the good things that
you earn and of what We have brought forth for you out of
the earth, and do not aim at giving in charity that which is
bad, while you would not take it for yourself unless you
connive at it, and know that Allāh is Self-sufficient,
Praiseworthy.[284]

Only they are charitable whom God has granted wisdom, while
niggardliness is devilish:

The devil threatens you with poverty and enjoins you to be
niggardly, and Allāh promises you forgiveness from Himself
and abundance; and Allāh is Ample-giving, Knowing: He
grants wisdom to whom He pleases, and whoever is granted
wisdom, he indeed is given abundant wealth; and none mind
but men of understanding.[285]

Charity may be exercised openly, as for some national good, or
secretly, as the helping of the poor:

If you give charity openly, it is well; and if you hide it and
give it to the poor, it is better for you; and this will do away
with some of your evil deeds; and Allāh is Aware of what
you do.[286]

The charity of a Muslim is not limited to his co-religionists:

To make them walk in the right way is not incumbent on
thee, but Allāh guides aright whom He pleases; and
whatever good thing you spend, it is to your own good; and
you do not spend but to seek Allāh's pleasure; and whatever

---

283. 2:262-264   284. 2:267   285. 2:268, 269   286. 2:271

good things you spend shall be paid back to you in full, and
you shall not be wronged.[287]

Charity must be exercised specially towards those who abstain
from begging:

> Charity is for the poor who are confined in the way of Allāh
> — they cannot go about in the land; the ignorant man thinks
> them to be rich because they abstain from begging; thou
> canst recognize them by their mark: they do not beg of men
> importunately; and whatever good thing you spend, Allāh
> knows it.[288]

The Prophet changed the Muslim mentality, so far as the
possession of wealth was concerned. The Muslim could possess
wealth but in his wealth others had a right too. Speaking of the
righteous, the Holy Quran says:

> They used to sleep but little of the night; And when morning
> came, they were (still) asking forgiveness. And in their
> property is a portion due to him who begs and to him who is
> deprived (of the fortunes of life).[289]

> Those who are constant at their prayers, And those in whose
> wealth there is a fixed portion, for him who begs and for him
> who is deprived.[290]

Prayer and charity were thus the two essential conditions of
righteousness, according to the Prophet. The portion referred to here
is different from *zakāt* which, being obligatory, leviable at a fixed
rate and the due of the State, is a kind of tax. The Prophet himself
made this clear:

> In one's wealth there is a due besides zakāt.[291]

All the wealth which a man earned was not his own. A part of it
should go to charity, however stringent the circumstances in which
a man himself lives. "Charity is incumbent on every Muslim,"[292] was
his clear order. But what about him who has not got anything? asked

---

287. 2:272　　　　288. 2:273　　　　289. 51:17-19　　　290. 70:23-25
291. Mishkāt, 6:6　　　　　　　292. Bukhārī, 24:30

asked his companions. He replied: "He should work with his hand and profit himself and give in charity." They again asked, If he has nothing in spite of this? The reply was: "He should help the distressed one who is in need." And if he is unable to do this, they said again. He said:

He should do good deeds and refrain from doing evil — this is charity on his part.[293]

The Prophet's conception of charity was the broadest possible:

On every bone of the fingers, charity is incumbent every day. One assists a man in riding his beast or in lifting his provisions to the back of the animal, this is charity; and a good word and every step which one takes in walking over to prayer is charity.[294]

Removal from the way of that which is harmful is charity.[295]

Even to meet a fellow-being with a cheerful countenance was charity:

Every good deed is charity, and it is a good deed that thou meet thy brother with a cheerful countenance and that thou pour water from thy bucket into the vessel of thy brother.[296]

The Prophet thus wanted to make men realize that to be charitable was to be a man. To make men prayer-minded and to make them charity-minded are the two distinctive characteristics of the religious system which he established.

293. Bukhārī, 24:31   294. Mishkāt, 6:6   295. Bukhārī, 46:24
296. Mishkāt, 6:6

Chapter 8
Character Building

One of the earliest works to which the Prophet applied himself was the building up of character. His heart ailed, as we have already seen, for the physical ills of humanity; the slave, the widow, the orphan, the needy, the one in distress, the oppressed and the wronged, had a very high place in his heart, and he would do what he could to help them and to make others feel for them as he himself felt. But moral considerations had a still higher place in his programme of reformation, and long before he introduced any reforms in regard to social relations, sex problems and state polity, he was engaged in the moral uplift of man. All wrongs had to be redressed, later on, by means of laws and regulations, but he was aware that even good laws could benefit humanity only when they were worked out by men standing on a high moral plane. It was, therefore, at Mecca and in very early days that, while introducing the high ideals of One God and One Humanity and applying himself to lead men to prayer and charity, he was equally devoted to raising men to a very high moral level.

The Prophet was recognized by friend and foe as the most truthful of men. When Abū Bakr was told that his friend Muḥammad claimed to have received revelation from on High, he remarked that he must be true in his claim because a man who had never uttered a falsehood against men could not utter a falsehood against God. It was in the very early days of his mission, when he received the commandment to warn his "nearest relatives,"[297] that he called out all the different families of the Quraish, now his opponents, at Mount Ṣafā; and when they had all gathered together, he asked them if they would believe him if he told them that a mighty army was lying in

---

297. 26:214

98

wait at the back of the hill to attack them. They all replied with one voice:

> Yes, we would; we have never known anything but truth from thee.[298]

On another occasion, his chief opponents gathered together to come to an agreed decision as to what was wrong with the Prophet. All kinds of questions were freely asked and answered. Was he a soothsayer? Was he a dreamer? Was he a poet? Was he a liar? And the answer to this last question was unamimous: "We have never known him tell a lie."

Still later, when opposition was at its highest and the Quraish were at war with the Prophet, Heraclius called Abū Sufyān, the Quraish leader of opposition, who was then in Syria for trading purposes, and asked him several questions regarding the Prophet. One of these questions was:

> Did you ever blame him for telling a lie before he said that he was a Prophet?

Abū Sufyan's reply was, "No."[299]

Himself so eminently truthful — and it was in fact on account of his truthfulness that he was called *al-Amīn* (the Faithful one) by his compatriots — he laid stress on truth as the basis of a high character:

> Surely truth leads to virtue, and virtue leads to paradise, and a man continues to speak the truth until he becomes thoroughly truthful; and surely falsehood leads to vice and vice leads to the fire, and a man continues to tell lies until he is written down a great liar with Allāh.[300]

He laid the basis of a society in which everyone was required to enjoin truth upon those with whom he came in contact, and to undergo every kind of suffering for the sake of truth:

---

298. Bukhārī, 65-26:2   299. *Ibid.*, 1:1   300. *Ibid.*, 78:69

Surely man is in a state of loss, Save those who believe and
do good works, And exhort one another to truth and exhort
one another to endurance.[301]

Ja'far, describing the Prophet's teachings before the Negus, said:

God raised a Prophet for our reformation ... He called us to
the worship of God ... He enjoined us to speak the truth, to
make good our trusts, to respect ties of kinship and to do
good to our neighbours.

With truth, falsehood could be challenged and vanquished:

Nay, We cast the truth against the falsehood so that it breaks
its head, and lo! it vanishes.[302]

The truth has come and falsehood is a vanishing thing.[303]

Truth was to be adhered to at all costs, even if it went against
one's own interests or the interests of one's friends and relatives:

O you who believe! Be maintainers of justice, bearers of
witness for Allāh's sake, though it be against your own
selves or your parents or near relatives; if he be rich or poor,
Allāh is most competent to deal with both; do not follow
your low desires lest you deviate; and if you swerve or turn
aside, Allāh is surely Aware of what you do.[304]

The principle of truth was not to be deviated from, even if it went
in favour of an enemy:

O you who believe! Be upright for Allāh, bearers of witness
with justice, and let not hatred of a people incite you not to
act equitably; act equitably, that is nearer to piety, and fulfil
your duty to Allāh; Allāh is aware of what you do.[305]

And even if one was called upon to speak truth in the face of a
tyrant, he must do it:

The most excellent jihād is the uttering of truth in the
presence of an unjust ruler.[306]

---

301. 103:2, 3   302. 21:18   303. 17:81   304. 4:135
305. 5:8   306. Mishkāt, 17

Only truth shall benefit in the final judgment:

> This is the day when their truth shall benefit the truthful ones; they shall have gardens beneath which rivers flow to abide in them for ever. Allāh is well-pleased with them and they are well-pleased with Allāh; this is the mighty achievement.[307]

The Prophet enjoys the distinction that he made people walk in the ways which he pointed out. The quality of truthfulness was so ingrained in the hearts of his followers that they not only loved truth but underwent the severest hardships for the sake of truth. When about two centuries later, the critics laid down certain canons to judge the truthfulness of the transmitters of the Ḥadīth, they all agreed on one point, that no companion of the Prophet had ever uttered a deliberate falsehood. In fact, one of the lastest revelations of the Holy Quran itself bears evidence to this:

> Allāh has endeared the faith to you and has made it beautiful to your hearts, and He has made unbelief and transgression and disobedience hateful to you.[308]

Faith includes all virtues taught by the Prophet, and truthfulness was one of the most prominent of these. Earlier, when the Prophet's companions were fleeing to Medina to escape the persecutions of the Quraish at Mecca, the Quran bore testimony to their truthfulness in the following words:

> And they who do not bear witness to what is false, and when they pass by what is vain, they pass by nobly.[309]

Perseverance was another characteristic which shone prominently in the life of the Prophet. Persecuted on all sides, suffering the severest hardships, with no apparent prospects of succcess, he stood adamant when threatened with death. "Uncle," he said, addressing Abū Ṭālib who had hitherto stood between him and the Quraish, but who now wavered, saying that the responsibility was becoming too heavy for him, "Should they place the sun in my right

---

307. 5:119   308. 49:7   309. 25:72

hand and the moon in my left in order to make me renounce this mission, I would not do it. I will never give it up until it shall please Allāh to make it triumph or I perish in the attempt."

Later, when temptations were offered, headship of the state, wealth and beauty, he spurned these and stood as firm as a mountain in the cause of the great reform to which he had set himself. Hemmed in narrowly for three years, he suffered all privations, but his faith was still as unshaken as ever. At the flight to Medina, hidden in the cave with a search party at its very mouth when a mere glance into the cave would have been sufficient to end his life, he still consoled his single companion, Abū Bakr, with the words: "Do not grieve, Allāh is surely with us."[310]

Next to truth, the Prophet laid stress on the quality of perseverance. These two qualities are combined in a short chapter which I have already quoted, ch. 103 of the Holy Quran: "They exhort one another to truth and they exhort one another to endurance."

Perseverance in the cause of truth brought down angels from heaven to console a man:

> Those who say, Our Lord is Allāh, then remain firm on the right way, the angels descend upon them, saying, Fear not, nor be grieved, and receive good news of the garden which you were promised:

> We are your guardians in this world's life and in the Hereafter, and you shall have therein what your souls desire and you shall have therein what you ask for.[311]

It is the state of mind of the companions that is depicted in the following words:

> And what reason have we that we should not rely on Allāh, and He has indeed guided us in our ways? And we would bear with patience your persecution of us; and on Allāh should the reliant rely.[312]

---

310. 9:40   311. 41:30, 31   312. 14:12

Patience and perseverance were inculcated again and again in the early revelations as well as in the later ones:

> To this then go on inviting, and go steadfastly in the right way as thou art commanded, and do not follow their low desires; and say, I believe in what Allāh has revealed of the Book and I am commanded to do justice between you.[313]

> Continue then in the right way as thou art commanded, as also he who has turned (to God) with thee ... And do not incline to those who are unjust, lest the fire touch you.[314]

Patience and prayer are stated to be the two doors through which Divine help comes:

> O you who believe! Seek assistance through patience and prayer for Allāh is with the patient.[315]

> Be patient, surely the good end is for the righteous.[316]

> O you who believe! Be patient and vie with one another in endurance and remain steadfast, and fulfil your duty to Allāh that you may be successful.[317]

The persecution which the Prophet's companions had to undergo, combined with the faith that their sufferings were in the cause of truth, developed the quality of perseverance in them to such a high degree that they considered no difficulty insurmountable.

Courage was another great quality on which stress was laid. The heart in which there was fear of God could not entertain fear of others than God, and this made the Muslims fearless in the face of the severest opposition:

> Those to whom the people said, Men have gathered against you, so fear them; but this increased their faith and they said, Allāh is Sufficient for us and most excellent is the Protector. So they returned with favour from Allāh and His grace; no evil touched them and they followed Allāh's pleasure, and

313. 42:15   314. 11:112, 113   315. 2:153   316. 11:49
317. 3:200

Allāh is the Lord of mighty grace. It is only the devil that causes you to fear from his friends, so do not fear them, and fear Me if you are believers.[318]

Fear not; surely I am with you: I do hear and see.[319]

And I do not fear in any way those you set up with Him ... And how should I fear what you have set up with Him while you do not fear that you have set up with Allāh that for which He has not sent down any authority to you.[320]

Those who deliver the messages of Allāh and fear Him and do not fear any one but Allāh; and Allāh is sufficient to take account.[321]

Those who say, Our Lord is Allāh, then continue on the right way, they shall have no fear nor shall they grieve.[322]

Now surely the friends of Allāh, they shall have no fear nor shall they grieve.[323]

It was on account of their fearlessness and great moral courage that even without the weapons which the enemy possessed, they were told to fight double their numbers:

If there are a hundred patient ones of you, they shall overcome two hundred, and if there are a thousand they shall overcome two thousand by Allāh's permission, and Allāh is with the patient.[324]

But when they grew stronger in arms and as well-equipped as the enemy, they could fight ten times their number:

If there are twenty patient ones of you, they shall overcome two hundred, and if there are a hundred of you they shall overcome a thousand of those who disbelieve.[325]

Actually the Muslims fought against three times their number on the field of Badr, against four times their number on the field of Uḥud, and against ten times their number in the battle of the Allies,

---

318. 3:173-175   319. 20:46   320. 6:80, 81   321. 33:39
322. 46:13   323. 10:62   324. 8:66   325. 8:65

and they won the battle on all these occasions. And in the battles which they had to fight against Persia and the Roman Empire, their numbers bore no comparison with the enemy forces, and they were almost always victorious. The courage which they showed on the battle-fields was in fact due to their faith.

But while facing so boldly all opposition to the cause of truth, they were also required to develop the quality of humility:

> And do not go about in the land exultingly, for thou canst not cut through the earth, nor reach the mountains in height. All this — the evil of it is hateful in the sight of thy Lord.[326]

> And do not turn thy face away from people in contempt, nor go about in the land exulting overmuch; surely Allāh does not love any self-conceited boaster. And pursue the right course in thy going about and lower thy voice.[327]

> Thus does Allāh set a seal over the heart of every proud, haughty one.[328]

> Surely He does not love the proud.[329]

> And seek assistance through patience and prayer, and surely it is a hard thing except for the humble ones.[330]

Humility became, in fact, deeply rooted in their hearts by the five daily prayers when all standing on terms of perfect equality bowed down before their Lord and prostrated themselves as one body. The Prophet's own example was a beaconlight to them in this respect. In his dealings with others he never placed himself on a higher pedestal. He was their spiritual guide and their ruler, but he was just one of them, being true to his picture as portrayed in the Holy Quran: "I am only a mortal like you." Out in the wood with his companions the time came for the preparation of food. Everybody was allotted a piece of work, and the spiritual and temporal overlord of all undertook the picking up of fuel. He would never scold a servant for

---

326. 17:37, 38   327. 31:18, 19   328. 40:35   329. 16:23
330. 2:45

doing a thing or for not doing a thing. A Jew to whom he owed some money addressed him very harshly and rudely while he was sitting with his companions: "You Banū Hāshim, never pay back when you once get something out of another." Instead of being offended with him, he paid him more than his due.

Selflessness was another great quality with which the Prophet armed his followers to fight the battle of life. God's pleasure was to be the only motive of one's actions, not one's gain or loss:

> And no one has with him any boon for which he should be rewarded, except the seeking of the pleasure of his Lord, the most High.[331]

> Say, My prayer and my sacrifice and my life and my death are all for Allāh, the Lord of the worlds.[332]

> And hear and obey and spend, ... And whoever is saved from the greediness of his soul, these it is that are the successful.[333]

> They prefer others before themselves though poverty may afflict them, and whoever is preserved from the niggardliness of his soul, these it is that are the successful ones.[334]

> And among men is he who sells himself away to seek the pleasure of Allāh, and Allāh is Affectionate to His servants.[335]

Great stress was laid on faithfulness to agreements and trusts:

> And those who are keepers of their trusts and their covenant.[336]

> And fulfil the promise, for every promise shall be called in question.[337]

> O you who believe! Fulfil the obligations.[338]

---

331. 92:19, 20   332. 6:162   333. 64:16   334. 59:9

335. 2:207   336. 23:8; 70:32   337. 17:34   338. 5:1

> And fulfil the covenant of Allāh when you have made a covenant, and do not break the oaths after making them fast, and you have indeed made Allāh a surety for you.[339]

Nations are particularly enjoined to fulfil their agreements, because they it is who, intoxicated with power, treat agreements as scraps of paper:

> And be not like her who unravels her yarn, disintegrating it into pieces after she has spun it strongly. You make your oaths to be means of deceit between you because one nation is more numerous than another nation.[340]

True to the spirit of these teachings, the Prophet and his followers stood firmly by their agreements under the most trying circumstances. There is not a single instance on record in which they broke their agreement with any other nation. A very critical situation arose under the truce of Ḥudaibiya. The agreement had just been signed, when Abū Jandal, a refugee from Mecca, appeared on the scene. He was a convert to Islām and had, on this account, been severely persecuted at Mecca. He showed the scars of his tortures to the Muslims. Under the conditions of the agreement, the Muslims could not give him shelter. The Prophet was moved and tried to secure an exception to the rigorous condition, but the other party did not agree to this, and Abū Jandal had to be sent back to his persecutors to be dealt with as they liked.

In the time of 'Umar, the Muslim general, Abū 'Ubaida, was obliged to evacuate the occupied territory of Ḥims, which the enemy was now going to occupy; and he ordered that the tax received from the people as a condition for their protection should be paid back to them because the Muslims could not afford them protection any longer. Another example of such scrupulous regard for agreements can hardly be met with elsewhere.

One of the evils to which man falls a prey easily is sexual indulgence. The Prophet's own chastity is testified by his severest

---

339. 16:91   340. 16:92

critics. Muir's remarks have already been quoted. And chastity was one of the rare virtues on which he laid great stress. Fornication was pointed out to be one of the three heinous sins:

> And they who do not call upon another god with Allāh, and do not slay the soul which Allāh has forbidden except in the requirements of justice, and who do not commit fornication.[341]

One was to keep at a safe distance from fornication:

> And go not nigh to fornication; surely it is an indecency and evil is the way.[342]

He further pointed out the ways by walking in which a man could guard against falling into this evil. He directed both sexes to keep their looks cast down when in the presence of each other:

> Say to the believing men that they cast down their looks and guard their chastity; that is purer for them; Allāh is Aware of what they do. And say to the believing women that they cast down their looks and guard their chastity.[343]

But women were further required not to make a display of their beauty or ornaments:

> And do not display their ornaments, except what appears thereof, and let them wear their head-coverings over their bosoms.[344]

Thus in the case of women it was deemed necessary that they should keep covered all parts of the body excepting the face and the hands which it was customary and natural to uncover. Those who could not find the means to marry were required to adopt other methods of keeping their passions in control:

> And let those who do not find the means to marry keep chaste until Allāh makes them free from want out of His grace.[345]

---

341. 25:68   342. 17:32   343. 24:30, 31   344. 24:31
345. 24:33

The quality of sincerity was to be developed by being first sincere in obedience to God:

> And they are not enjoined anything except that they should serve Allāh, being sincere to Him, upright.[346]

> Serve Allāh, being sincere to Him in obedience; now surely sincere obedience is due to Allāh alone.[347]

Hypocrisy was condemned in the severest terms:

> Surely the hypocrites are in the lowest stage of the fire, and thou shalt not find a helper for them.[348]

> They were on that day much nearer to unbelief than to belief. They say with their mouths what is not in their hearts.[349]

All qualities which make man stand on a high moral plane were inculcated one after another. Thankfulness was one of them:

> And when your Lord made it known, if you are thankful I will certainly give you more; and if you are ungrateful, My chastisement is truly severe.[350]

> Eat of the good things We have provided you with, and give thanks to Allāh if He it is that you serve.[351]

> If you are ungrateful, then surely Allāh is Self-sufficient, above all need of you, and He does not like ungratefulness in His servants; and if you are grateful, He likes it in you.[352]

One was required to be grateful to men as well. The Prophet said:

> Whoever is not thankful to men is not thankful to Allāh.

Thankfulness to men meant repaying their kindness:

> Is the reward of goodness aught but goodness.[353]

Social virtues were taught and evils which arise from ease and comfort were denounced:

---

346. 98:5   347. 39:2, 3   348. 4:145   349. 3:167
350. 14:7   351. 2:172   352. 39:7   353. 55:60

O you who believe! Let not one people deride another
people, perchance they may be better than they; nor let
women deride other women, perchance they may be better
than they; and do not find fault with your people, nor call
one another by nicknames; evil is a bad name after faith; and
whoever does not turn (to the right course), these it is that
are the unjust.

O you who believe! Avoid most of suspicion, for suspicion
in some cases is a sin; and do not spy, nor let some of you
backbite others. Does one of you like to eat the flesh of his
dead brother? You abhor it.[354]

The high morals depicted in the Holy Quran were the morals of
the Prophet, and it was in this shape that he wanted to mould the
character of his followers. Even a cursory glance at the lives of his
first four successors, Abū Bakr, 'Umar, 'Uthmān and 'Alī, men who
were the rulers of a vast empire, would show that the Prophet
achieved a mighty success in this respect. I may quote only one
description of the high moral plane on which the Prophet's
companions stood:

And the servants of the Beneficent God are they who walk
on the earth in humbleness, and when the ignorant address
them, they say, Peace.
And they who pass the night prostrating themselves before
their Lord and standing.
And they who, when they spend, are neither extravagant nor
parsimonious, and keep between these the just mean.
And they who do not call upon another god with Allāh and
do not slay the soul which Allāh has forbidden except in the
requirements of justice and who do not commit fornication
...
And they who do not bear witness to what is false, and when
they pass by what is vain, they pass by nobly.

---

354. 49:11, 12

And they who, when reminded of the communications of their Lord do not fall down thereat, deaf and blind.

And they who say, Our Lord! Grant us in our wives and our offspring the joy of our eyes, and make us a guide for the righteous.

They shall be rewarded with high places because they were patient, and shall be offered therein greetings and salutations.[355]

---

355. 25:63-75

Chapter 9
Wealth

The Prophet aimed, from the first, at establishing a world-wide order affecting all phases of human life. The foundations of this order rested on two main principles, a vital faith in one God and the oneness of humanity. After adopting the necessary methods for deepening the roots of God-consciousness in the human heart and welding together diverse races and nations into one human nation, the Prophet applied himself to the working out of the essential details of that order. In any order relating to human life, the question of wealth undoubtedly occupies a very prominent place, and this question finds a detailed discussion in the Prophet's teachings. All questions affecting the acquisition of wealth, its possession and its proper distribution are fully discussed. In the first place, wealth was not a thing to be discarded, nor was its acquisition prohibited. Nature's gifts were the gifts of God:

> Say, Who has prohibited the adornment of Allāh and the good provisions which He has brought forth for His servants? Say, These are for the believers in the life of this world, purely theirs on the Resurrection-day; thus do we make the communications clear for a people who know. Say, My Lord has prohibited only indecencies, those of them that are apparent as well as those that are concealed.[356]

> O you who believe, Eat of the good things that We have provided you with, and give thanks to Allāh if He it is that you serve.[357]

> And He it is Who produces gardens of vine, trellised and untrellised, and palms and seed-produce, of which the fruits

---

356. 7:32, 33   357. 2:172

112

are of various sorts, and olives and pomegranates, like and unlike; eat of its fruit when it bears fruit and pay the due of it on the day of its reaping ... And of cattle He created beasts of burden and those which are fit for slaughter only; eat of what Allāh has given you.[358]

And He it is Who has made the sea subservient that you may eat fresh flesh from it and bring forth from it ornaments which you wear, and thou seest the ships cleaving through it and that you might seek of His bounty and that you may give thanks.[359]

The Prophet even taught his followers to pray to God for the good things of this life:

Our Lord! Grant us good in this life and good in the Hereafter.[360]

The possession of wealth was further pointed out to be a necessary condition of life on this earth:

And do not give away your wealth, which Allāh has made for you a means of support to the weak of understanding and maintain them out of the profits of it.[361]

Wealth was thus a means of support for man; its wastage had to be guarded against, and those who were likely to squander away their wealth had to be restrained from doing so by placing their wealth in the control of guardians who were required to maintain them out of its profits. It had to be earned and acquired and men and women were in this respect placed on one level:

Men shall have the benefit of what they earn and women shall have the benefit of what they earn.[362]

Wealth could also be acquired by inheritance, and men and women were again placed on the same level:

358. 6:141, 142   359. 16:14   360. 2:201   361. 4:5
362. 4:32

Men shall have a portion of what the parents and the near relatives leave, and women shall have a portion of what the parents and the near relatives leave.[363]

It could also be acquired as a gift:

But if they (that is, the women) of themselves be pleased to give you a portion of it, then eat it with enjoyment and with wholesome result.[364]

The only restriction on the acquisition of wealth was that it could not be acquired by unlawful means:

And do not swallow up your wealth among yourselves by false means, neither seek to gain access thereby to the judges, so that you may swallow up a part of the wealth of men wrongfully while you know.[365]

O you who believe! Do not devour your wealth among yourselves falsely except that it be trading by your mutual consent.[366]

The companions of the Prophet did all kinds of work; they were engaged in trade; they cultivated land; they carried on different professions; they worked as labourers; but they were enjoined not to be so engrossed with these occupations as to forget their duty to God:

Men whom neither merchandise nor selling diverts from the remembrance of Allāh and the keeping up of prayer and the giving of poor-rate.[367]

O you who believe! When the call is given for prayer on Friday, hasten to the remembrance of Allāh and leave off business; that is better for you if you know. And when the prayer is ended, disperse abroad in the land and seek of Allāh's grace, and remember Allāh much so that you may be successful.[368]

---

363. 4:7   364. 4:4   365. 2:188   366. 4:29
367. 24:37   368. 62:9, 10

O you who believe! Let not your wealth and your children divert you from the remembrance of Allāh; and whoever does that, these are the losers.[369]

The possession of wealth was subject to the same condition; there was nothing wrong in having wealth but wealth was not to be placed above duty to God:

Say, If your fathers and your sons and your brethren and your mates and your kinsfolk, and the wealth which you have acquired, and trade, the dullness of which you fear, and the houses which you love, are dearer to you than Allāh and his Messenger and striving in His way, then wait till Allāh brings about His command, and Allāh does not guide the transgressing people.[370]

It did not matter if a man had more or less of wealth. Inequality in wealth was just a condition of life. There is inequality throughout nature:

And in the earth there are tracts side by side and gardens of grapes and corn and palm trees having one root and others having distinct roots — they are watered with one water and We make some of them excel others in fruit; surely there are signs in this for a people who understand.[371]

Dost thou not see that Allāh sends down water from the cloud, then We bring forth therewith fruits of various sorts; and in the mountains are streaks, white and red, of various hues, and others intensely black. And of men and beasts and cattle are various sorts of it likewise.[372]

There is variety throughout; no two blades of grass are alike, nor are any two men alike. There are differences in their brains, in their capacity for work, in their environment and in the circumstances in which they have to work, and therefore also in the fruit which they reap for their work. These differences could not be obliterated, and

---

369. 63:9   370. 9:24   371. 13:4   372. 35:27, 28

men were therefore told to accept them as one of the conditions of life:

> We distribute among them their livelihood in the life of this world, and We have exalted some of them above others in degrees that some of them may take others in subjection.[373]

> And Allāh has made some of you excel others in the means of subsistence, so those who are made to excel do not give away their subsistence to those who are under them that they should be equal therein.[374]

But it was impressed on the minds of both the rich and the poor that the possession of more wealth did not raise the dignity of a man, nor did poverty degrade him. Such turns of fortune did not count as anything with God, nor should they count with those who believed in Him:

> Then, as for man, when his Lord tries him and gives him wealth and makes him lead an easy life, he says, My Lord has honoured me. And when He tries him and straitens to him his means of subsistence, he says, My Lord has disgraced me. By no means![375]

> And were it not that all people would become one (disbelieving) community, we would certainly have assigned to those who disbelieve in the Beneficent God to make of silver the roofs of their houses and the stairs by which they ascend, And the doors of their houses and the couches on which they recline, And of gold; and all this is naught but provision of this world's life, and the higher life is with thy Lord only for those who have regard for their duty.[376]

> The most honourable of you with Allāh is the one among you who has the greatest regard for his duty.[377]

---

373. 43:32   374. 16:71   375. 89:15, 16   376. 43:33-35
377. 49:13

The Prophet himself, who was honoured both as the spiritual and temporal head of the people, had not any wealth in his house, and he did not leave a single coin to be inherited. The mentality he wanted to create was that wealth was not a criterion of greatness or honour. He viewed the question of wealth in its right perspective; it was needed for the subsistence of man but its possession did not raise the dignity of man.

Wealth was necessary for man to live on this earth, but it was only a means to an end; not the end. There were higher values of life and these were not to be lost sight of in the pursuit of wealth:

> The mercy of thy Lord is better than what they amass.[378]

> The love of desires, of women and sons, and hoarded treasures of gold and silver, and well-bred horses and cattle, and tilth, is made to seem fair to men; this is the provision of the life of this world; and Allāh is He with Whom is the good goal of life. Say, Shall I tell you of what is better than these? For those who have regard for their duty are gardens with their Lord in which rivers flow to abide in them and pure mates and Allāh's pleasure ... The patient and the truthful and the obedient and those who spend in charity and those who ask for Divine protection in the morning times.[379]

In the following verse, as also in some other places, the hereafter stands for the higher life or the higher values of life:

> Whoever desires this present life (i.e. makes wealth the goal of his life), We hasten to him therein what We please for whomsoever We desire ... And whoever desires the hereafter (i.e. makes the higher life his goal) and strives for it as he ought to strive and he is a believer, their striving shall be gratefully accepted. All do We aid - these as well as those - out of the bounty of thy Lord, and the bounty of thy Lord knows no bounds. See how We have made some of

---

378. 43:32   379. 3:14-17

them to excel others, and certainly the hereafter is much superior in respect of degrees and much superior in respect of excellence.[380]

On the other hand, the amassing of wealth led to some evils, which are repeatedly pointed out. In the first place, inordinate love of wealth diverts a man from the higher values of life:

The desire of increasing riches diverts you, until you come to the graves.[381]

A man who runs madly after wealth, whose avarice for possessions of more and more wealth knows no limits, cannot devote any attention to the higher values of life. There is no place for the love of God in a mind in which the love of wealth reigns supreme, and by and by he forgets God altogether and loses the contentment of mind, which can be found only in the remembrance of God:

Those who believe and whose hearts are set at rest by the remembrance of Allāh; now surely, by Allāh's remembrance are the hearts set at rest.[382]

The love of wealth, if no check is put upon it, ultimately becomes a burning fire in the heart:

Woe to every slanderer, defamer, Who amasses wealth and considers it a provision (to keep off evils); He thinks that his wealth will make him abide. Nay! he shall certainly be hurled into the crushing disaster. And what will make thee realize what the crushing disaster is? It is the fire kindled by Allāh, Which rises above the hearts. It shall be closed over upon them, In extended columns.[383]

Love of wealth is here spoken of as becoming first a fire that burns in the heart, and then this very fire turns into hell in the next life. The lover of wealth is here called a slanderer and defamer; elsewhere it is stated that the love of wealth ultimately leads to the basest morals:

---

380. 17:18-21   381. 102:1, 2   382. 13:28   383. 104:1-9

And obey not any mean swearer, Defamer, going about with slander, Forbidder of good, transgressor, sinful, Greedy; besides all that, mischiefmonger; Because he is possessed of wealth and sons.[384]

The Prophet thus made it clear that inordinate love of wealth leads to moral degradation of the worst type. It further kills all noble feelings for the service of humanity:

But you do not honour the orphan; Nor do you urge one another to feed the needy; And you eat away the heritage with devouring greed; And you love wealth with exceeding love.[385]

The amassing of wealth is therefore condemned in the severest words:

Those who hoard up gold and silver and do not spend it in Allāh's way, announce to them a painful chastisement. On the day when it shall be heated in the fire of hell, then their foreheads and their sides and their backs shall be branded with it; This is what you hoarded up for yourselves, therefore taste what you hoarded.[386]

To keep man's desire for wealth within bounds, and as a measure against wealth accumulating in fewer and fewer hands, in other words, to guard men against the evils of capitalism, the Prophet, guided by Divine revelation, laid down certain laws. Every religious reformer laid stress on charity and so did the Prophet, as already shown, but he went a step further. He made charity compulsory under certain conditions. What a man earned was the fruit of his labour and he was entitled to it. But he owed a duty to his fellow-beings. When he had spent what he needed out of his earnings and saved a certain amount, this saving was treated as taxable capital, and a fixed portion of this saving was to be collected and spent, under an organized system, for the benefit of the poor and the needy.

---

384. 68:10-14   385. 89:17-20   386. 9:34, 35

Charity was thus to be exercised in two ways, a voluntary charity out of one's income and an obligatory charity out of one's savings.

The obligatory charity was called *zakāt*, meaning *an act of purification*. The amassing of wealth was regarded as carrying a certain degree of uncleanness with it, becuase it affected the heart of man with the love of wealth. This uncleanness could be washed off by giving away every year one-fortieth of it for the benefit of the poor. Hence it was called *zakāt*. Though obligatory, the basic idea underlying zakāt was man's own conviction that the amassing of wealth was an impure act, and that purification could only be effected by paying 2 ½ per cent out of it for the benefit of the poor.

It was undoubtedly a tax, but a tax which had a moral sanction behind it. As such it stands unique both as charity and as tax. As charity it is obligatory, but the obligation is moral. As tax, the sanction behind it is moral, not the physical force of the State. Zakāt was, however, not simply obligatory charity; it was a State institution; and in the absence of a Muslim State, a national institution. The individual was not at liberty to calculate and spend his zakāt as he liked, or to give a certain portion of his wealth to deserving persons. He was required to contribute the same to a fund which was to be used for the uplift of the community. Collectors were to be appointed for the realization of this tax and their wages were a burden on this very fund. Thus it was laid down:

> Obligatory charity is meant only for the poor and the needy and the officials appointed for its collection and those whose hearts are made to incline to truth and the ransoming of captives and those in debt and for the cause of Allāh and the wayfarer.[387]

The Prophet thus aimed at destroying the evils of capitalism, not capitalism itself. He did not interfere with private ownership of industry and property, nor did he deprive a man of the fruits of his labour. He left an open field for competition, for hard work and for the exercise of intelligence. He tried to bring about a just distribution

---

387. 9:60

of wealth by requiring the capitalists, the possessors of wealth, to give away a part of their wealth for the benefit of the less favoured members of society. By so doing, he in fact laid the foundations of a social system in which the number of capitalists went on increasing, so that competition being widened as much as possible might be healthier. The poorer members of the community were able to start business with a small capital provided from the zakāt fund, and then to increase it by their own diligence and hard work. Wealth which has a tendency to get into fewer and fewer hands was thus made accessible to wider and wider circles.

Zakāt was not, however, the only means by which it was sought to bring about a proper distribution of wealth. A law of inheritance was also laid down by which the wealth of one man was distributed at his death among many. The Prophet introduced a two-fold reform into the laws of inheritance as existing in his time. He made the female a co-sharer with the male, and he ordered the division of property among all the heirs on a democratic basis. One big capitalist was thus replaced by many small capitalists at every Muslim's death. The general law is thus laid down in the Holy Quran:

> Men shall have a portion of what the parents and the near relatives leave, and women shall have a portion of what the parents and near relatives leave, whether there is little of it or much.[388]

Under this general law, details were laid down that the property of the deceased person should go to daughters as well as to sons, to mothers as well as to fathers, to wives and to husbands, to brothers and to sisters, and so on. The heirs were divided into two groups, the first group consisting of children, parents and husband or wife, and the second consisting of brothers and sisters and other distant relatives. All the persons in the first group were immediate sharers, and if all of them were living they had all of them a right in the property of the deceased. The members of the second group inherited if all members of the first group or some of them were wanting. Both

---

388. 4:7

groups were capable of further extension; grandchildren or still lower descendants taking the place of children, grandparents or still higher ascendants taking the place of parents, and uncles and aunts and other distant relatives taking the place of brothers and sisters.

Another remedy for the evils of capitalism was the regulation of the relations between the debtor and the lender. Faithfulness to agreements being one of the primary duties of a Muslim, the debtor was required to be faithful in repaying the debt:

> Amongst the best of you are those who are good in payment of debt.

> Whoever contracts a debt intending to repay it, Allāh will pay it for him; and whoever contracts a debt intending to waste it, Allāh will bring him to ruin.[389]

> Delaying the payment of debt by a well-to-do person is injustice.[390]

> Deferring payment by one who has the means to pay legalizes his punishment.[391]

But if the debtor was in straitness, the lender was required to be lenient, even to the extent of foregoing the debt:

> If the debtor is in straitened circumstances, then there should be postponement until he is in ease; and if you remit it as alms, it is better for you if you know.[392]

This principle was worked out most liberally by the Prophet as the head of the Muslim State:

> I am nearer to the believers than themselves, so whoever of the believers dies and leaves a debt, its payment is on me; and whoever leaves property, it is for his heirs.[393]

A debt contracted for a right cause was thus to be paid by the State, if the debtor was unable to pay it. A still greater remedy for the evils of capitalism was, however, applied in the form of the

---

389. Bukhārī, 43:2   390. Bukhārī, 43:12   391. Ibid., 43:13
392. 2:280   393. Bukhārī, 39:5

prohibition of usury. The Holy Quran deals with this subject after devoting two sections to the importance of charity, for inasmuch as charity is the broad basis of human sympathy, usury annihilates all sympathetic feelings. The usurer is described thus:

> Those who swallow usury cannot arise except as one whom the devil has prostrated by his touch does arise.[394]

Such is, in fact, the usurer who would not hesitate to reduce the debtor to the last straits if thereby he might add a penny to his millions. It is on account of his selfishness and greed for money that he is spoken of as being unable to arise.

In the great struggle between capital and labour that has always been going on in the world, the Prophet sided with labour:

> Allāh has allowed trade and forbidden usury.[395]

While trading requires the use of labour and skill and elevates the morals, usury promotes habits of indolence, cunning and oppression. Hence it was laid down that trade was allowed but usury was prohibited.

Another arrangement to minimize the evils of capitalism in the social order established by the Prophet was the injunction relating to bequests. Everyone who left considerable wealth to be inherited was required to make a bequest for charitable objects to the maximum extent of one-third of his property:

> Bequest is prescribed for you when death appproaches one of you, if he leaves behind wealth for parents and near relatives, according to usage, a duty incumbent upon those who have a regard for duty.[396]

The Prophet also stressed the making of bequest in his sayings:

> It is not right for a Muslim who has property regarding which he must make a will that he should sleep for two nights (consecutively) but that his will should be written down with him.[397]

---

394. 2:275   395. 2:275   396. 2:180   397. Bukẖārī, 55:1

That this will was for charitable objects, and therefore limited to one-third of the property, is shown by what is related by Sa'd, the conqueror of Persia. He said:

> The Messenger of Allāh used to visit me at Mecca in the year of the Farewell pilgrimage, on account of my illness which had become very severe. So I said, My illness has become very severe and I have much property and there is none to inherit me but a daughter. May I then bequeath two-thirds of my property as a charity. He said, No. I said, Half. He said, No. Then he said: Bequeath one-third and one-third is much, for if thou leave thy heirs free from want, it is better than that thou leave them in want begging of other people; and thou dost not spend anything seeking thereby the pleasure of Allāh but thou art rewarded for it, even for that which thou puttest into the mouth of thy wife.[398]

To sum up, the Prophet's viewpoint regarding wealth was that both men and women should earn it because it was the means of their support, that it could be possessed but its possession did not raise the dignity of man, and that the amassing of wealth led to its love and the love of wealth led to moral debasement; and he, therefore, based his economic system on the democratic principles of zakāt, the division of property at death among the heirs, and the prohibition of usury. He did not abolish capitalism but he remedied its evils; he did everything to widen the circle of small capitalists to make competition healthier and increase the wealth of the nation as a whole.

---

398. Bukhārī, 23:36

Chapter 10
Work and Labour

One of the greatest services which the Prophet rendered to humanity was to give an impetus to work and to dignify labour. The principle was laid down at the very start in the most unequivocal terms that no one who does not work should hope to reap any fruit and that the worker should have his full reward:

> That man shall have nothing but what he strives for; And that his striving shall soon be seen; Then shall he be rewarded for it with the fullest reward.[399]

> So whoever does good works and he is a believer, there shall be no denying of his effort, and We write it down for him.[400]

As the work is, so is the fruit:

> Your striving is surely directed to various ends. Then as for him who gives to others and is dutiful, and accepts the best (principles); Surely We will facilitate for him the easy end. And as for him who withholds from others and considers himself free from need, And rejects the best (principles), We will facilitate for him the difficult end. And his wealth will not avail him when he perishes.[401]

> Faces on that day shall be happy, Well-pleased because of their striving.[402]

> This is a reward for you and your striving shall be recompensed.[403]

---

399. 53:39-41   400. 21:94   401. 92:4-11   402. 88:8, 9
403. 76:22

And all have degrees according to what they do. And thy
Lord is not heedless of what they do.[404]

It was not only his followers whom the Prophet told to work and
to hope for nothing but the fruit of their work; he repeatedly drew the
attention of his opponents to the same principle:

O my people! Work according to your ability, I too am
working.[405]

Equal stress is laid throughout the Holy Quran on faith and work;
"those who believe and do good" is the ever-recurring description of
the faithful. In fact, faith without work is expressly stated to be of no
use:

On the day when some of the signs of thy Lord come, its
faith shall not profit a soul which did not believe before, or
earn good through its faith.[406]

The Prophet himself was an indefatigable worker. While he
passed half the night, and even two-thirds of it, praying to God, he
was doing every kind of work in the day-time. No work was too low
for him. He would milk his own goats, he would dust his house; he
would tie his camel and look after it personally. He would assist his
wife in her household duties. In person he would do shopping, not
only for his own household but also for his neighbours and friends.
He worked like a labourer in the construction of the mosque. Again,
when a ditch was being dug round Medina to fortify it against a
heavy attack, he was seen at work among the rank and file. He never
despised any work, however humble, notwithstanding the dignity of
his position as Prophet, as generalissimo and as king. He thus
demonstrated through his personal example that every kind of work
dignified man, and that a man's calling, whether high or low, did not
constitute the criterion of his status. A roadside labourer, a hewer of
wood and a drawer of water were as respectable members of the
social order founded by the Prophet as a big merchant or a high
dignitary.

---

404. 6:132   405. 6:135; 11:93, 121; 39:39   406. 6:158

Here are some of his sayings:

> No one eats better food than that which he eats out of the work of his own hand.[407]

> Allāh did not raise a prophet but he pastured goats.

And in answer to a question whether he did it, he replied:

> Yes! I used to pasture them for the people of Mecca for some carats.[408]

He made it clear that every work was honourable in comparison with asking for charity:

> If one of you should take his rope and bring a bundle of firewood on his back and then sell it, with which Allāh should save his honour, it is better for him than that he should beg of people, whether they give him or do not give him.[409]

The most honourable of his companions did not disdain the work of a porter. Abū Mas'ūd said:

> When the Messenger of Allāh commanded us to give in charity, one of us went to the market and carried a load for which he got a small measure of grain, and some of them are millionaires to-day.[410]

The humblest work carried with it a dignity; those who followed the profession of a butcher or a seller of meat, a goldsmith, a blacksmith, a tailor, a weaver or a carpenter were looked upon as honourable members of society.[411]

The relations between a labourer and his employer were those of two contracting parties on terms of equality. The Prophet laid down a general law relating to contracts:

> Muslims shall be bound by the conditions which they make.[412]

---

407. Bukhārī, 34:15
408. Ibid., 37:2
409. Ibid., 24:50
410. Ibid., 24:10   411. Ibid., 34:21, 28-32
412. Bukhārī, 37:14

The master and the servant were considered two contracting parties, and the master was as much bound by the terms of the agreement as the servant. This was made plain by the Prophet:

> Allāh says, There are three persons whose adversary in dispute I shall be on the day of Resurrection: a person who makes a promise in My name then acts unfaithfully, and a person who sells a free person then devours his price, and a person who employs a servant and receives fully the labour due from him then he does not pay his remuneration.[413]

No service carried with it any indignity, so much so that it was recommended that the servant may eat on the same table with his master.[414]

If the remuneration of a labourer was left unpaid, its investment in some profitable business was recommended, the servant being entitled to the profits. In a long Ḥadīth it is related that three men were overtaken with a severe affliction, from which God delivered them because of some good which each had done. One of these was an employer who invested a servant's unpaid remuneration in a profitable business:

> And the third man said, I employed labourers and I paid them their remuneration with the exception of one man - he left his due and went away. So I invested his remuneration in a profitable business until it became abundant wealth.[415]

The Ḥadīth goes on to say that when after a long time the labourer came back for the remuneration, the employer made it over to him along with all the profit which it had brought.

The employees of the State, its collectors and executive officers and its judges, were all included in the category of servants. They were entitled to a remuneration but they could not accept any gift from the public. Even those who taught the Quran were entitled to remuneration:

---

413. Bukhārī, 34:106　　　　414. *Ibid.*, 49:18　　415. *Ibid.*, 37:12

The most worthy of things for which you take a remuneration is the Book of Allāh.[416]

'Umar was once appointed a collector by the Prophet, and when he was offered a remuneration he said that he did not stand in need of it. The Prophet, however, told him to accept it and then give it away in charity if he liked.[417] The principle was thus laid down that every employee, every servant, every labourer was entitled to a remuneration.

Trading was one of the most honourable professions and the Prophet laid special stress on it:

The truthful, honest merchant is with the prophets and the truthful ones and the martyrs.[418]

People were taught to be generous in their dealings with one another:

May Allāh have mercy on the man who is generous when he buys and when he sells and when he demands his due.[419]

The man who "used to give respite to the one in easy circumstances and forgive one who was in straitened circumstances" was forgiven because of this good deed.[420]

Honesty was to be the basic principle in all dealings:

If they both speak the truth and make manifest (the defect, if any, in the transaction), their transactions shall be blessed, and if they conceal (the defect) and tell lies, the blessing of their transaction shall be obliterated.[421]

The taking of oaths was forbidden:

The taking of oaths makes the commodities sell but it obliterates the blessing therein.[422]

Speculation, in cereals especially, was strictly prohibited:

---

416. Bukhārī, 37:16   417. *Ibid.*, 94:17   418. Tirmidhī, 12:4
419. Bukhārī, 34:16   420. *Ibid.*, 34:17   421. *Ibid.*, 34:19
422. *Ibid.*, 34:26

Whoever buys cereals, he shall not sell them until he obtains their possession.[423]

Trade was to be carried on for the benefit of the public, and the withholding of stocks was forbidden:

Whoever withholds cereals that they may become scarce and dear is a sinner.[424]

The cultivation of land and planting of trees was encouraged:

There is no Muslim who plants a tree or cultivates land, then there eat of it birds or a man or an animal but it is a charity for him.[425]

Whoever cultivates land which is not the property of anyone, has a better title to it.[426]

Those who had vast tracts of land, which they could not manage to cultivate for themselves, were advised to allow others to cultivate them free of charge:

If one of you gives it (i.e. cultivable land) as a gift to his brother, it is better for him than that he takes for it a fixed payment.[427]

But it was allowed that the owner of the land should give it to others to cultivate for a share of the produce or for a fixed sum.[428] The ownership of land by individuals was thus recognized, as also their right to buy or sell it or to have it cultivated for them by others. A warning was at the same time given that a people who give themselves up entirely to agriculture, neglecting other lines of their development, could not rise to a position of great glory. It is related that the Prophet said when he saw a plough and some other agricultural implements:

This does not enter the house of a people but it brings ingloriousness with it.[429]

423. Bukhārī, 34:54
424. Mishkāt, 12:8 425. Bukhārī, 41:1
426. *Ibid.*, 41:15
427. Mishkāt, 12:13
428. Bukhārī, 41:8, 11, 19
429. *Ibid.*, 41:2

Chapter 11
Home Life

More important even than the economic problem was, in the Prophet's estimation, the problem of the home. The home is the unit of human society, and the sum total of human happiness is ordinarily determined by the happiness which prevails in the home. The stability of the home is also an index to the stability of the society and its civilization. As the male and the female together make the home, it was necessary to bring about a right understanding of their positions and relations.

Woman, before the time of the Prophet, was generally regarded as a slave. Barring exceptional cases she was not considered a person in the sense in which man was a person. A person is, in the first place, one who can own property but the woman could not own any property or carry on any transaction in her own name. On the other hand, she was herself the property of her husband. It was a perfect revolution in the existing social order which the Prophet brought about by making woman the owner of property, a person in the real sense of the word.

In the earliest revelations of the Prophet, man and woman are spoken of as standing on the same level in the sight of God:

> Consider the night when it draws a veil, And the day when it shines in brightness, And the creating of the male and the female.[430]

> And that He it is Who causes death and gives life, And that He created pairs, the male and the female, From the small life-germ when it is adapted.[431]

Both the male and female were made perfect:

---

430. 92:1-3   431. 53:44-46

Was he not a small life-germ in the seminal elements? Then he was a clot of blood, so He created him and made him perfect. Then He made of him two kinds, the male and the female.[432]

Offspring is spoken of as God's gift, and as such the female had precedence:

He grants to whom He pleases daughters and grants to whom He pleases sons; Or he makes them of both sorts, male and female.[433]

Later revelation develops the same basic idea:

O people! Be careful of your duty to your Lord Who created you from a single being and created its mate of the same kind, and spread from these two many men and women.[434]

It was also in the earlier revelation that it was made clear that spiritually the woman stood on the same level with the man:

And whoever does good deeds, whether male or female, and he is a believer, these shall enter the garden.[435]

Whoever does good, whether male or female, and he is a believer, We will make him live a happy life, and We will give them their reward for the best of what they did.[436]

Women were also spoken of as receiving Divine revelation, the greatest spiritual gift:

And We revealed to Moses' mother, saying, Give him suck; then when thou fearest for him, cast him into the river, and do not fear or grieve.[437]

They were chosen by God and purified as men were chosen and purified:

And when the angels said, O Mary! Allāh has chosen thee and purified thee.[438]

---

432. 75:37-39   433. 42:49, 50   434. 4:1   435. 40:40
436. 16:97   437. 28:7   438. 3:42

The Prophet's wives are spoken of as having been thoroughly purified:

> Allāh only desires to keep away the uncleanness from you, O people of the household! and to purify you a thorough purifying.[439]

And generally women are spoken of as equal to men in all spiritual aspects:

> The men who submit to Allāh and the women who submit, and the men who believe and the women who believe, and the men who obey and the women who obey, and the men who are truthful and the women who are truthful, and the men who persevere and the women who persevere, and the men who are humble and the women who are humble, and the men who are charitable and the women who are charitable, and the men who fast and the women who fast, and the men who are chaste and the women who are chaste, and the men who remember Allāh much and the women who remember — Allāh has prepared for them protection and a mighty reward.[440]

The Prophet, however, went further and introduced a reform by which the woman became a free person in the fullest sense of the word. She was no more the property of another person; she could earn property, she could own property, she could inherit property, she could transfer property, she could give property as a gift and she could receive property as a gift. The social system founded by the Prophet thus brought about a revolution in the position of the woman, removing the bondage of half the human race. In the first place, she could earn money; she could do any work she liked, and she was entitled to the fruit of her labour just as man was:

> Men shall have the benefit of what they earn and women shall have the benefit of what they earn.[441]

---

439. 33:33   440. 33:35   441. 4:32

This direction opened for her all vocations, and though her maintenance by the husband was a condition of marriage, she could support herself and even become the bread-winner of the family, if she stood in need of it. She could also inherit property. The Arabs had a very strong tradition against inheritance by women because they could not fight in defence of their tribe. The Prophet had a new message for her:

> Men shall have a portion of what the parents and the near relatives leave, and women shall have a portion of what the parents and the near relatives leave.[442]

According to the details of the law of inheritance laid down by the Prophet, the wife inherited the husband, the mother inherited along with the father, the daughter along with the son, the sister along with the brother, the aunt along with the uncle, and so on. Again, woman could deal with her property as she liked in her personal right; she could sell it or she could give it as a gift;

> But if the women of themselves be pleased to give to you a portion of it, then eat it with enjoyment and with wholesome result.[443]

> O Muslim women! Let not a neighbour despise for her neighbour a gift, even though it be the trotters of a goat.[444]

Every woman was in fact made the owner of some property at her marriage. No marriage was legal unless the woman had some property settled on her. This was a practical step to raise the woman to the status of the man:

> Lawful for you are all women besides this, provided that you seek them with your property, taking them in marriage, not committing fornication. Then as to those whom you profit by (by marrying), give them their dowries as appointed.[445]

Marriage even with non-Muslim women was not allowed unless the dowry was paid, and the woman was made the owner of property:

---

442. 4:7   443. 4:4   444. Bukhārī, 51:1   445. 4:24

And the chaste from among the believing women and the chaste from among those who have been given the Book before you are lawful for you when you have given them their dowries, taking them in marriage, not fornicating nor taking them for paramours in secret.[446]

There was no limitation to the amount of dowry, a whole estate or a heap of gold could be settled on her:

If ... you have given one of them a heap of gold, take not from it anything.[447]

The woman was recognised as a free person by making her the owner of property at marriage, but even before marriage she was recognized as such, as she could be taken in marriage only with her permission or consent. The Prophet is reported to have said:

The widow shall not be married until she is consulted, and the virgin shall not be married until her consent is obtained.[448]

Where a woman was given in marriage against her wishes, the marriage was annulled by the Prophet.[449] In the Holy Quran, it is laid down in clear words:

It is not lawful for you that you should take women as a heritage against their will.[450]

In fact, marriage was recognized as a sacred contract, and there could be no contract without the consent of the two parties:

And they (your wives) have made with you a firm covenant.[451]

For the stabilization of society, every man and every woman was required to live in a married condition. There is a clear injunction to this effect:

And marry those among you who are single.[452]

---

446. 5:5 447. 4:20 448. Bukhārī, 67:42
449. *Ibid.*, 67:43 450. 4:19 451. 4:21 452. 24:32

The Prophet is reported to have said to certain people who talked of fasting in the day-time and keeping awake during the night praying to God, and keeping away from marriage:

> I keep a fast and I break it, and I pray and I sleep, and I am married; so whoever inclines to any other way than my way (Sunna), he is not of me.[453]

On another occasion, he said:

> O assembly of young people! Whoever of you has the means to support a wife, he should get married; this is the best means of keeping the looks cast down and guarding chastity; and he who has not the means, let him keep fast, for this will act as castration.[454]

The Prophet is also reported to have said that "the man who marries perfects half his religion."

Marriage was thus recognized as a means to the moral uplift of man, and such it is in fact. Mutual love between husband and wife - a love based not on momentary passion but on a life long connection - and the consequent parental love for offspring leads to a very high development of the feeling of love of man for man as such, and this in its turn leads to the disinterested service of humanity. Through marriage the home is made a training ground for the development of the feeling of love and service. Here a man finds a real pleasure in suffering for the sake of others, and the sense of service is thus gradually developed and broadened.

Marriage was no more a hindrance in the spiritual progress of man and in his perfection; it was rather a help and led to the development of the spiritual faculties and to perfection:

> And one of His signs is that He created mates for you from yourselves that you might find quiet of mind in them, and He put between you love and compassion.[455]

---

453. Bukhārī, 67:1 454. *Ibid.*, 67:2   455. 30:21

The women are an apparel for you and you are an apparel for them.[456]

Marriage, as already noted, was, according to the Prophet, a contract; it is expressly called a mīthāq (contract) in the Holy Quran.[457] But owing to the importance of the rights and obligations to which it gave rise, the mutual responsibilites of the husband and the wife and their joint responsibility for bringing up the children, special importance was attached to this contract. In the first place, it was necessary that the assent of both parties to it should be made in a public place and should be made publicly known:

Make public this marriage and perform it in the mosques and beat drums for it.[458]

Clandestine transactions were classed as fornication. In addition to publicity, a sacred character was given to the contract by the delivery of a sermon before the announcement of the marriage. The sermon was meant not only to give a religious character to the contract, but also to remind the pair that their happiness in life depended on their respect for thir mutual rights and obligations under the contract.

The wife was recognized as having rights against her husband, similar to those which the husband had against the wife:

And the wives have rights similar to their obligations in a just manner.[459]

The position of the wife in the family was, according to the Prophet, that of a ruler:

Everyone of you is a ruler and everyone shall be questioned about his subjects; the king is a ruler, and the man is a ruler over the people of his house, and the woman is a ruler over the house of her husband and his children.[460]

To one of his companions he is reported to have said:

---

456. 2:187   457. 4:21   458. Mishkāt, 13:4 459. 2:228
460. Bukhārī, 67:91

Thy body has a right over thee and thy soul has a right over thee and thy wife has a right over thee.[461]

The husband was required to provide for the maintenance of the wife and for her lodging according to his means:

Men are the maintainers of women.[462]

Let him who has abundance spend out of his abundance, and whoever has his means of subsistence straitened to him, let him spend out of that which Allāh has given him.[463]

Lodge them where you lodge, according to your means.[464]

The wife was bound to keep company with her husband, to preserve the husband's property from loss or waste and to refrain from doing anything which should disturb the peace of the family. She was required not to admit anyone into the house whom the husband did not like and not to incur expenditure of which the husband disapproved.[465]

Stress was laid on kindly and good treatment of the wife. "Keep them in good fellowship,"[466] "Treat them kindly"[467] is the oft-recurring advice, so much so that kindness was recommended even if a man disliked his wife:

And do not straiten them in order that you may take part of what you have given them unless they are guilty of manifest indecency, and treat them kindly; and if you dislike them, it may be that you dislike a thing while Allāh has placed abundant good in it.[468]

Good treatment towards the wife was a criterion of good morals:

The most excellent of you is he who is best in his treatment of his wife.[469]

And again:

---

461. Bukhārī, 67:90   462. 4:34   463. 65:7
464. 65:6   465. Bukhārī, 67:87   466. 2:229
467. 4:19   468. 4:19   469. Mishkāt, 13:11-ii

Accept my advice in the matter of doing good to women.[470]

The Prophet's parting advice to his followers, when addressing them at the Farewell pilgrimage, was:

> O my people! You have certain rights over your wives and so have your wives over you ... They are the trust of Allāh in your hands. So you must treat them with all kindness.[471]

Notwithstanding the sacredness of the character of the marriage-tie, the necessity was recognized of keeping the way open for its dissolution. But this right was to be exercised only under exceptional circumstances. The Prophet allowed divorce but he did not like it:

> Never did Allāh allow anything more hateful to Him than divorce.[472]

> With Allāh, the most detestable of all things allowed is divorce.[473]

The Holy Quran too, while allowing divorce, discourages it:

> If you hate them (i.e., your wives), it may be that you dislike a thing while Allāh has placed abundant good in it.[474]

The mentality which the Prophet aimed at creating among his followers was that of facing the difficulties of married life along with the enjoyment of its comforts, and of avoiding the disruption of the family relations as long as possible, turning to divorce only as a last resort.

The principle of divorce and its procedure was laid down in the following words:

> And if you fear a breach (Ar. _shiqāq_) between the two, then appoint a judge from his people and a judge from her people; If they both desire agreement, Allāh will effect

---

470. Bukhārī, 67:81   471. Muslim, 15:19
472. Abū Dāwood 13:3   473. _Ibid._   474. 4:19

harmony between them; surely Allāh is Knowing, Aware.[475]

The other alternative is referred to further on, thus:

And if they separate, Allāh will render them both free from want out of His ampleness, and Allāh is Ample-giving, Wise.[476]

Thus not only was the principle of divorce laid down but also the process to be adopted when a rupture of marital relations was feared. The principle of divorce spoken of here is _shiqāq_ or a disagreement to live together as husband and wife. In this respect, the two sexes are placed on a level of perfect equality. A "breach between the two" implies that either the husband or the wife wants to break off the marriage agreement, and hence either may claim divorce. All causes of divorce are made subject to the condition that one of the parties cannot pull together with the other and wants a divorce. No defect in the husband or the wife is in itself a reason for divorce unless one of the parties is desirous of terminating the union. The process to be adopted lays down clearly that the husband has not the right to break off the tie when and how he likes. Judges must be appointed to settle the dispute, and the husband and the wife are again placed on the same level by each of them being represented by a person of his or her choice. The judges are told to try to bring about a reconciliation in the first place, and resort to divorce is only to be had when all means of reconciliation have been exhausted.

The wife's right of divorce was clearly established in the case of Jamīla, who came to the Prophet demanding a divorce from her husband Thābit ibn Qais, saying: "O Messenger of Allāh! I do not find fault in Thābit ibn Qais regarding his morals or faith but I cannot pull together with him" Being asked if she would return to him the orchard which he had settled upon her as a dowry, she replied in the affirmative, and the Prophet ordered her husband to take back his orchard and divorce her.[477]

---

475. 4:35   476. 4:130   477. Bukhārī, 68:12

The Prophet recognized, as a rule, only the union of one man and one woman as a valid form of marriage, but in exceptional circumstances he allowed the man to have more wives than one, up to the limit of four; but under no circumstances could the woman have more husbands than one. This was in keeping with his claim that his religion was the religion of nature. While marriage was recognized by the Prophet as the union of two natures which are one in their essence, the object of marriage was the multiplication of the human race:

> The Originator of the heavens and the earth; He made mates for you from yourselves ... multiplying you thereby.[478]

> And Allāh has made wives for you from yourselves, and has given you sons and daughters from your wives.[479]

Nature's arrangement in this respect is that while one man can raise children from more wives than one, one woman can have children at one time only from one husband. Therefore while polygamy could under certain circumstances be a help for the welfare of society, polyandry had no conceivable use for man. The Quranic verse permitting polygamy in certain circumstances occurs in the fourth chapter of the Holy Quran, and runs thus:

> If you fear that you cannot act equitably towards orphans, then marry such women as seem good to you, two, three and four.[480]

It is evident that there is some connection between the two parts of this verse, not acting equitably towards orphans and taking in marriage more wives than one. This connection is made clear further on in this chapter with special reference to this verse:

> That which is recited to you in the Book, is concerning the orphans of women to whom you do not give what is appointed from them - and you are not inclined to marry them - nor to the weak among the children.[481]

---

478. 42:11   479. 16:72   480. 4:3   481. 4:127

The two verses read together show that when a widow was left with orphans to bring up, she and her children did not get any share of inheritance; nor were people inclined to marry widows who had children on account of the burden which it involved of bringing up the children. For the relief of distress of widows and orphans, therefore, two reforms were introduced by the Prophet. As already pointed out, the widow and the orphan were given their share of inheritance, and now a limited polygamy was allowed to provide a home for the widow. The home was to the Prophet the source from which sprang up the great qualities of love and service, and through love and service other great and noble qualities, and he did not shrink from providing half a home if a full home was not possible. Half a home was after all a home, and far better than no home.

The fourth chapter, in which this permission finds a place, was revealed at a time when the Muslims were compelled to carry on incessant war against an enemy bent upon their extirpation. The bread-winners had all to take the field against the enemy, and many of them were lost in the unequal battles that were being fought by the small Muslim band against overwhelming forces. Women had lost their husbands and young children their fathers, and the number of widows and orphans was daily increasing. To provide for the excess number of women, and for the proper bringing up of the orphans under parental care and affection, the Prophet, guided by Divine revelation, permitted a limited polygamy. This meausure further afforded protection for the chastity of the widows who would otherwise have fallen a prey to moral depravity. Such a measure was also needed to keep up the numerical strength of a community whose numbers were fast dwindling, owing to the slaugher of large numbers in warfare. Polygamy was thus allowed in exceptional circumstances when the strict rule of monogamy was calculated to bring hardship on society, both physically and morally. The only alternative in such a case would have been to allow prostitution, but this was abhorrent to the Prophet, and he regarded it as the greatest degradation for woman.

Chapter 12
The State

The universality of the prophet's message lay in two, or rather in three, directions. In the first place, he claimed to be a Guide for all nations of the world. This, in fact, was a clear implication of the great idea of the oneness of humanity on which he based his religion. Thus he was commanded:

> Say, O people! I am the messenger of Allāh towards you all.[482]

> We have not sent thee but as a mercy for the nations.[483]

Another offshoot of the same basic idea was that he claimed to be a Guide for all time, so that it was laid down that religion was made perfect by his appearance and that no prophet would appear after him:

> This day have I perfected your religion for you and completed My favour on you and chosen for you Islām as a religion.[484]

> Muhammad is not the father of any of your men but he is the Messenger of Allāh and the last of the prophets, and Allāh is Cognizant of all things.[485]

The second peculiarity of his message was that it aimed at the development of human nature in its entirety, the cultivation of each of its numerous faculties. There was no phase of human life in which he did not claim to furnish guidance. In his own life, every phase of human activity found a thorough manifestation. He was born an orphan and brought up by his uncle; in his youth he earned his livelihood by labour and hard work, including the pasturing of goats;

---

482. 7:158   483. 21:107   484. 5:3   485. 33:40

later on he took to trade and had to go abroad for this purpose; he married and had children to look after; he championed the cause of the widow, the orphan, the weak and the oppressed, while still a young man; on receiving the Call he applied himself whole-heartedly to reform the rampant evils, and underwent the severest persecutions and hardest trials of a reformer; he had to fly for his very life to a distant place where he had to organize people belonging to different races and different religions into a compact whole; he had to defend a small and helpless community against overwhelming forces bent on its destruction; he had to lead his followers personally into the field of battle to face the enemy and to the mosque to make them bow before God; he had to declare war and to make peace; he was a soldier as well as a general; he was a law-giver as well as a judge; he led the life of a recluse passing his nights praying to God till his feet were swollen, and that of a man of the world passing his days in the worldly engagements of his growing community; and lastly, he became the head of a State which within ten years after his death was the greatest living empire of the world.

The Prophet was thus not only the founder of a religion which has gone on expanding for fourteen centuries, but also the founder of a State, branches of which are even now spread over the world. He, however, not only founded a State but also laid down the rules and laws by which a good State should be governed. The State which the Prophet founded was invested with physical force, as every State must necessarily be, to fulfil its function of stopping aggression and oppression, but it was one of the unique services which he rendered to humanity that he spiritualized this greatest of all human physical forces. Like the religion which he founded, his ideal for a State was democratic, but it was a democracy based upon the fear of God and upon responsibility to God in the first place. The following descriptions of believers occurring in one of the early revelations, when he was still leading the life of a helpless and persecuted reformer, shows how the two ideas of democratizing and spiritualizing the State were blended:

And those who respond to their Lord and keep up prayer and their government is by counsel among themselves and who spend out of what We have given them.[486]

The chapter in which this verse occurs is entitled _Shūrā_, or Counsel, on account of the great democratic principle of counsel laid down here as the basis of the future State of Islām.

But the verse itself gives prominence to the great acts that are needed to spiritualize man, answering the call of God, praying to God and devoting oneself to the service of humanity. The verses that follow show that the Prophet wanted his followers to be trained on spiritual lines while preparing them for conducting the affairs of the State:

And those who, when great wrong afflicts them, defend themselves. And the recompense of evil is punishment proportionate thereto, but whoever forgives and amends (matters thereby), he shall have his reward from Allāh; for He does not love the unjust. And whoever defends himself after his being oppressed, these it is against whom there is no way of blame. The way of blame is only against those who oppress men and revolt in the earth unjustly - these shall have a painful chastisement. And whoever is patient and forgiving, that surely is an affair the doing of which should be determined upon.[487]

These excellent rules for the defence of the Muslim community which was being oppressed and persecuted at the time, and for the forgiveness of the enemy that was bent upon its extirpation, clearly show that the basis was herein being laid of a Muslim State, because forgiveness could only be exercised towards a vanquished enemy. It was in their sufferings that the Muslims were being told to exercise forgiveness when their turn should come to take revenge on a fallen enemy. The passion for revenge was thus being obliterated from their hearts from the very beginning, and the physical force of the State was spiritualized by making it subject to moral considerations.

---

486. 42:38   487. 42:39-43

In forming a State, some men had necessarily to be placed in authority over others, but those placed in authority were warned that they would be answerable to God, first of all, for what they did in the exercise of authority. The warning to David was a warning to every true believer:

> O David! We have made thee a ruler in the land, so judge between men with justice and do not follow (thy) desire, lest it should lead thee astray from the path of Allāh; for those who go astray from the path of Allāh; shall have a severe chastisement because they forget the day of reckoning.[488]

The day of reckoning had to be borne in mind when exercising authority over others. The Prophet also told his followers in plain words that if they were placed in authority over others, their responsibility to God became the greater, and they could not be saved if they did not work whole-heartedly for their good:

> There is not a man whom Allāh grants to rule people, then he does not manage their affairs for their good but he will not smell the sweet odour of paradise.[489]

When bidding farewell to two of his govenors, who were leaving Medina to take charge of two provinces, his last words were:

> Be gentle to the people and be not hard on them, and make them rejoice and do not incite them to aversion.[490]

It was due to this moral training in the exercise of government that the Prophet's successors devoted themselves heart and soul to the good of the people over whom they were placed in authority. How the Commander of the Faithful felt his responsibility to God may be illustrated by two incidents in the history of 'Umar, the second Caliph. An ordinary citizen rebuked him in public, saying repeatedly: "Fear Allāh, O 'Umar!," Some people wanted to stop this rudeness, but 'Umar himself intervened, saying:

> Let him say so; of what use are these people if they do not tell me such things.

---

488. 38:26   489. Bukhārī, 94:8 490. *Ibid.*, 64:62

On another occasion, he visited a famine-stricken camp at night incognito, and finding a woman with no food to give her children, he rushed back to Medina, a distance of three miles, and took a sack of flour on his own back to feed the distressed woman and her children. When a servant offered his services to carry the load, he said:

> In this life you might carry my burden, but who will carry my burden on the day of judgement ?

The foundations of the State founded by the Prophet were thus spiritual. They were at the same time democratic in the truest sense of the word. All people, including the ruler, had equal rights and obligations and were subject to the same law. The Prophet himself did not claim any rights beyond those which other Muslims had. In the actual working of the State organization, of which he was the founder and the head, there was nothing to distinguish him from others. Outsiders came and asked: Which of you is Muḥammad? He was a King, yet he had no throne to sit upon, no crown to wear, no palace to live in, no bodyguard to protect him from enemies with whom he was carrying on an incessant war. The apartments in which he and his family lived were small mud huts without doors, while the furniture of his house was nothing but an earthen vessel for water and a rough mat to sleep on. He passed day after day and night after night without any fire being lit in his house to cook food for him and his family, and had nothing to live upon except dates and water. He never claimed any superiority on account of his being a ruler. When his soldiers were digging a ditch for the defence of Medina, he was there with his pick-axe, and when they were removing heaps of dust and stones, he was one of the labourers who were covered with dust. If ever there was a democracy free from all differences of heredity, rank or privilege, it was the democratic State of which the foundations were laid by the Prophet.

Every one was a subject and every one a ruler in the Islāmic State:

> Every one of you is a ruler and every one shall be questioned about those under his authority; the king is a ruler and he shall be questioned about his subjects, and the man is a ruler

over the people of his house and he shall be questioned
about those under his authority, and the woman is a ruler
over the house of her husband and she shall be questioned
about those under her authority, and the servant is a ruler so
far as the property of his master is concerned and he shall be
questioned about that which is entrusted to him.[491]

The law was one for all and all were one in the eye of the law,
including the Amīr, the man entrusted with the highest command,
and including the Prophet himself, who was as much subject to law
as any of his followers; "I follow naught but what is revealed to me;
indeed I fear the chastisement of a mighty day if I disobey my
Lord."[492]

The head of the Muslim State was also called an Imām, lit., *one
whose example is followed*, because he was expected to serve as a
model for others. The first Amīr, or the first successor of the Prophet,
was Abū Bakr, and the very first words in which he addressed those
who had sworn allegiance to him were:

Help me if I am in the right, set me right if I am in the
wrong.

And again:

The weak among you shall be strong in my eye till I have
vindicated his just rights, and the strong among you shall be
weak in my eye till I have made him fulfil the obligations
due from him.

The law was to be held supreme, the Caliph himself being
subject to the same law as those under him:

Obey me so long as I obey Allāh and His Messenger; in case
I disobey Allāh and His Messenger, I have no right to
obedience from you.

It was the Prophet who had laid down this rule of the supremacy
of the law:

491. Bukhārī, 11:11   492. 10:15

> To hear and obey (the authorities) is binding, so long as one is not commanded to disobey God; when one is commanded to disobey God, he should not hear or obey.[493]

The law of the Quran was supreme indeed, but there was no bar to making laws according to the needs of the people so long as they did not go against the spirit of the revealed law. On being appointed governor of Yemen, Mu'ādh was asked by the Prophet as to the rule by which he would abide. "By the law of the Quran," was the reply. "But if you do not find any direction therein," asked the Prophet. "Then I will act according to the Sunna of the Prophet," was the reply.

"But if you do not find any direction in the Sunna of the Prophet," he was again asked. "Then I will exercise my judgment and act on that," came the reply. The Prophet raised his hands and said:

> Praise be to Allāh Who guides the messenger of His Messenger as He pleases.[494]

The necessary laws were, however, to be made by consultation. In reply to 'Alī who enquired as to how to proceed in cases where there was no definite direction in the Holy Quran, the Prophet is reported to have said:

> Gather together the righteous from among my community and decide the matter by their counsel and do not decide it by one man's opionion.

Counsel was freely resorted to by the Prophet himself in all important matters. Medina was attacked thrice by the Quraish, and every time the Prophet held a consultation with his followers as to how to meet the enemy. On one of these occasions he acted on the opinion of the majority and marched out of Medina to meet the enemy, although his own opinion was that the Muslim army should not leave the town. He definitely directed his followers to take counsel whenever an important matter was to be decided: "Never do

---

493. Bukhārī, 56:108   494. Abū Dāwood, 23:11

a people take counsel but they are guided to the right course in their affair." When some people disobeyed his orders in one of the battles and this act of theirs caused heavy loss to the Muslim army, he was still commanded to take counsel with them: "pardon them and ask Divine protection for them and take counsel with them in affairs of the State."

It appears from the Holy Quran that people were gathered together for counsel on many important occasions:

> Only those are believers who believe in Allāh and His Messenger and when they are with him on a momentous affair, they go not away till they ask his permission.[495]

It was due to these clear directions to make the laws for themselves and to decide other important matters by counsel that the first successors of the Prophet had councils to help them in all such matters. It was also in the early history of Islām that great Imāms, such as Imām Abū Hanīfa, freely resorted to analogical reasoning in legislation, and *ijtihād* was recognized as a source of Islāmic law along with the Holy Quran and the Sunna of the Prophet. The two principles of democracy, the supremacy of the law and the taking of counsel in making new laws and deciding other important affairs, were thus laid down by the Prophet himself. The third principle of democracy, the election of the head of the State, was also recognized by him. He went so far as to say that even a Negro could become the head of the State, and that obedience was due to him as to any other head.[496] It was due to such teachings of his that the election of a head was the first act of his companions after his death. When news of his death spread, the Muslims gathered together and freely discussed the question as to who should succeed the Prophet as the head of the State. The Ansār, the residents of Medina, were of opinion that there should be two heads, one from among the Quraish and one from among themselves, but the error of this view was pointed out by Abū Bakr who made it clear in an eloquent speech that the State could have only one head[497]; and so Abū Bakr was

---

495. 24:62   496. Bukhārī, 10:54   497. Bukhārī, 62:6

elected, being, as 'Umar stated, "the best" of them and "the fittest of the Muslims to control their affairs."[498]

Fitness to rule was the only consideration to decide the election, and even a Negro could be elected to rule over the Arabs, as the Prophet had laid down in clear words: "Hear and obey though a Negro, whose head is like a raisin, is appointed to rule over you."[499]

People who could elect the head could also depose him in extreme cases if it became necessary, because the Prophet had laid down the condition to hear and obey "whether we liked or disliked, and whether we were in adversity or ease, even if our rights were not granted," and "the authority of the head could only be disputed if he committed open acts of disbelief in which you have a clear argument from Allāh."[500]

People were required to have the moral courage to point out the injustice of the rulers. The Prophet said:

> The most excellent ġihād is the uttering of truth in the presence of an unjust ruler.[501]

The public treasury was not the property of the head of the State; he was only entitled to a fixed salary like all other public servants. It was Abū Bakr, the very first successor of the Prophet, who acted on this rule.[502] They had no special privileges and he could be sued in a court like any other member of the Muslim community. The Prophet himself set the example by declaring on his death-bed that if anyone had any claim against him, he should come forward. 'Umar, the second successor of the Prophet, appeared as a defendant before one of his judges. The Prophet had no doorkeeper, and the governors were required to be accessible to all people at all hours of the day. 'Umar issued instructions to his governors that they should lead simple lives and should not keep a doorkeeper who should prohibit people from approaching them.

---

498. Bukhārī, 94:51   499. *Ibid.*, 10:54   500. *Ibid.*, 93:2
501. Mishkāt, 17   502. Bukhārī, 34:15

The Prophet did not introduce any compulsory taxation to carry on war with his enemies; people were required only to subscribe voluntarily if they felt the justice of the cause. He carried on war for seven years only on voluntary subscriptions. The only compulsory tax was the zakāt, collected annually at the rate of 2 1/2 per cent on the savings of the year, and the main item of its expenditure was the help of the poor and the needy. Later on 'Umar laid it down clearly that people could only be taxed with their assent and according to their capacity.[503] The State was required not only to provide for uncared-for families, but also to pay the unpaid debt of a deceased person when there were no other means to pay it.[504] As much regard was to be paid to the rights of non-Muslim subjects of the State as to those of the Muslims.[505]

Positions of authority were considered a trust, and the fittest persons were to be chosen for this purpose:

> Allāh commands you to make over trusts to those worthy of them and that when you judge between people you judge with justice.[506]

Justice was declared to be the foundation-stone of the State which the Prophet founded; in dealing equitably no distinction was to be made between friend and foe, between people whom one loved and those whom one hated:

> O you who believe! Be upright for Allāh, bearers of witness with justice; and let not the hatred of a people incite you not to act equitably: act equitably, that is nearer to piety; and be careful of your duty to Allāh, for Allāh is Aware of what you do.[507]

> O you who believe! Be maintainers of justice, bearers of witness for Allāh's sake, though it be against your own selves or your parents or near relatives; if he be rich or poor, Allāh is competent to deal with both; therefore do not follow

---

503. Bukhārī, 62:8 504. *Ibid.*, 43:11   505. *Ibid.*, 62:8   506. 4:58
507. 5:8

your low desires lest you deviate; and if you swerve or turn aside, Allāh is surely Aware of what you do.[508]

It was with his Flight to Medina, from which the Muslim Era starts, that the Prophet became the head of a State which was soon compelled to enter on warfare. Medina, as already stated, was attacked thrice by the Quraish, in the years 2, 3 and 5 of the Flight, and this war came practically to a close by the Prophet's conquest of Mecca in the year 8. This sequence of events shows that the Prophet was not aggressive. In fact, permission to fight was given to the Prophet after war was made on him, as clearly stated in the Holy Quran:

> Permission to fight is given to those upon whom war is made because they are oppressed.[509]

Even after permission was given, he was expressly told that his war was to be defensive.:

> And fight in the way of Allāh with those who fight with you, and do not exceed this limit.[510]

Though he had never fought during the fifty-four years of his earlier life, he acted as a most sagacious general, and did not allow a drop of the blood of his followers to flow in vain. He kept himself so well-informed about the enemy's movements that in the whole course of a continuous war of seven years, and in spite of the enemy strength, spread over the whole country, being overwhelmingly greater than the small Medina Muslim community, the enemy forces were never able to trap the Muslims unawares or to deal a crushing blow to them on any field. In the battles of Uḥud and Ḥunain, when defeat was almost in sight for the Muslim force, the Prophet warded off the danger by risking his own life and saved the situation. The Prophet had, up to the time that war began, trained his men only on spiritual lines, but when war actually started he did all that was necessary from a military point of view. He had a census taken of the men who could take the field against the enemy. He also made

---

508. 4:135   509. 22:39   510. 2:190

arrangements to train them in the use of arms. Even women were called upon to carry provisions,[511] to take care of the sick and the wounded,[512] to remove the wounded and the slain from the battlefield,[513] and to take part in actual fighting in extreme cases.[514]

War was enforced on the Prophet; temperamentally he was averse to it. He therefore tried his best to reduce its horrors to the lowest possible limit. Strict orders were given that noncombatants should not be killed in war. A woman was found among the killed in one of the battles, and when this fact was brought to his notice, "He forbade the killing of women and children" in war.[515] "She was not fighting," he said, and added that even hirelings should not be killed in war.[516] All noncombatants, including labour units employed in war, were thus exempted; and the battle was a trial of strength only between the fighting forces. War became necessary in order to save the Muslim community from extermination, but bloodshed was limited to the minimum.

It was due to the Prophet's abhorrence of unnecessary bloodshed that he was so generous in making peace. The cessation of hostilities was made necessary if the enemy desired peace:

> If they incline to peace, do thou also incline to it and trust in Allāh.[517]

The enemy's proposal of peace might be insincere; it might be made to gain time and prepare for another war; but even then the offer was not to be rejected. "And if they intend to deceive thee," the verse quoted above goes on to say "then surely Allāh is Sufficient for thee." The Prophet's faith in God was to him an assurance - even so was the faith of his followers - that even if the enemy made another war, he would again be defeated and would have to beg for peace. The righteousness of the cause was to him a sufficient guarantee that the upholders of that cause would be victorious in the end. The

---

511. Bukhārī, 56:66　　　　　512. *Ibid.*, 56:67　　513. Bukhārī, 56:68
514. *Ibid.*, 56:62, 63, 65　　515. *Ibid.*, 56:147　516. Mishkāt, 18:4
517. 8:61

instructions given to his troops show his anxiety to mitigate the horrors of war:

> In avenging the injuries inflicted upon us, molest not the harmless inmates of domestic seclusion; spare the weakness of the female sex; injure not the infant at the breast or those who are ill in bed. Abstain from demolishing the dwellings of the unresisting inhabitants; destroy not the means of their subsistence, nor their fruit trees, and touch not the palms.[518]

The treatment meted out to prisoners of war shows the same anxiety:

> So when you meet the disbelievers in war, smite their necks until you have overcome them, and made them prisoners. Afterwards either set them free as a favour or let them ransom themselves, until the war lays down its weapons.[519]

The Prophet actually set free all prisoners of war as a favour, except in the battle of Badr, when seventy prisoners of war were set free on paying ransom while war with the Quraish was still in progress. On one occasion, in the battle of Ḥunain, as many as six thousand prisoners were set free as a favour.

The war which the Prophet was compelled to fight was thus a mercy at its start because it had to be fought in self-defence; a people were to be saved from aggressors who were out to annihilate them. It was a mercy in the end because it had to be stopped when the aggressor sued for peace - safety of the oppressed being the object, not the annihilation of the aggressor. It was a mercy for the non-combatants as well who in modern warfare are greater victims of the tyranny of war than even the fighting forces. The aggressors were not to be annihilated because annihilation of the enemy was not the only means of stopping the aggression. The Prophet's viewpoint was that at times a generous peace was a better remedy for aggression than the

---

518. *The Spirit of Islām*, by Syed Amir Ali, p.81   519. 47:4

annihilation of the aggressor, because while an attempt to annihilate a people might only fan the fire of revenge among the vanquished, a generous peace might bring about a real change of heart.